Douglass College: A History

Mabel Smith Douglass, 1877–1933

Douglass College:
∿∿∿ A History

by George P. Schmidt

RUTGERS UNIVERSITY PRESS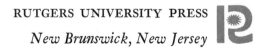
New Brunswick, New Jersey

To my colleagues and students

~~~ Preface

When Dean Ruth Adams asked me, in a letter in March of 1962, to write a history of Douglass College as a contribution to the approaching semi-centennial, I was happy to comply, for as a member of the faculty for thirty years I thought I knew something about the subject. As a matter of fact, Dean Margaret Corwin had informally suggested such a book several years earlier, and in my last year of teaching I had done some preliminary work on it, using released time arranged by Dean Mary Bunting. After my retirement in 1960 I dropped the project for other activities, but upon receiving Miss Adams' invitation went back to it and, with some interruptions, carried it through to completion. This meant several trips back to New Brunswick of from one to three months each, to gather material in the Douglass and Rutgers archives. The actual writing was done in Florida and Cape Cod, where I could see the College in better perspective than from the corner of George Street and Nichol Avenue.

The writer who tries to fashion history out of contemporary events in which he has had a part faces peculiar problems, as

Preface

Thucydides found out long ago. Without presuming to compare myself to Thucydides, I am aware that the dual role of participant and historian, while offering obvious advantages, also presents pitfalls. True, the person who was there can flesh in the dead bones of the official documents. When, for example, the secretary to the faculty records, in the chaste language of academe, that "after a discussion lasting almost an hour the motion was defeated," the writer, who helped defeat it, can brighten his narrative with some of the fireworks of that explosive hour. And when he encounters a fiery editorial in the files of the student newspaper he can convey, having been faculty adviser to the paper's staff that year, some of the pent-up emotions that produced it. If the result of all this is a somewhat informal history, I offer no apologies: I planned it that way. For it is my hope that former students or faculty colleagues who may read this book will then be able to say yes, that is how it was, that is the way I remember it.

But if vividness is a natural by-product of recalled participation, objectivity is not. When you have taken part, the chances are you have also taken sides, and your judgment of an event in retrospect is likely to be warped. Then, too, memory plays tricks and one person's unsupported recollection is a flimsy basis for dependable history. Taking all this into account, I buttressed my memory of events wherever possible with documentary evidence. I studied the minutes of the Faculty, the Trustees' Committee, and Government Association, and also the annual reports of the Dean and the reports of important committees. My best unofficial sources were *Campus News* and its successor, *Caellian*, both of which I read with care and discretion. I also examined the available letters and papers of Dean Mabel Smith Douglass, James Neilson,

Preface

Leonor F. Loree, and others. I interviewed many colleagues, both older and younger, as well as a number of alumnae, and checked my recollections against theirs. During my last stay on campus I sought out younger faculty members who had come to prominence since my retirement and also talked with several student leaders, to get the feel of the contemporary College. Whether an objective account has emerged from all these efforts, informed readers will have to decide for themselves. Factual errors have, I hope, been kept at a minimum, but no doubt some readers will differ with my interpretations.

The book could not have been written without the cooperation of a number of people. The entire College administration, from the Dean on down, was most helpful in finding places for me to stay and to work. The Douglass collection in the Library, the official records in College Hall, and Associate Alumnae files were all put to use, as were the Neilson, the Loree, and other papers in the Rutgers University Library. Frances E. Riche '32, Secretary of the College, was closely connected with the enterprise from beginning to end. She prepared data of many kinds for my use, read every chapter critically, was, in short, indispensable. Dean Edna M. Newby '31 smoothed my path by setting up interviews for me and also found time to read the entire manuscript. Dean Adams read early chapters too and made helpful suggestions. My colleague of many years in the History Department, Margaret A. Judson, during her year as Acting Dean, made it possible for me to bring the book up to date and secured the services of a research assistant, Elizabeth Tilton Welsh '43, who had been a history honors student and who helped materially with the gathering of data for the last chapters. Evelyn Bruno Finck '48 thoughtfully culled many sources for photographs to illustrate

~~~ Contents

Douglass College: A History

The Founding of the College

The visitor to New Brunswick driving down from New York or north Jersey catches his first glimpse of Douglass College when he emerges on the high-level bridge above the Raritan River and looks upstream. There, in a welcome setting of green after miles of highway grime and clutter, stand the principal College buildings, loosely grouped around the white spire of Voorhees Chapel. On his left, as he turns toward the town, the student residences of Gibbons campus wheel into view and beyond them Hickman Hall rises foursquare to the winds. Directly ahead looms the pink and white facade of the Music Building, crowning Sonomon's Hill. Farther on, Antilles Field stretches out inside its retaining wall; there the ground drops off sharply to the river and the old canal locks, where in another era the barges used to load for their leisurely journey into the interior. Ahead, in the curve of the river, lies New Brunswick. Four-lane Memorial Parkway sweeps around this curve today, but in the early years it was Burnet Street, a narrow, historically picturesque path through the oldest and shabbiest part of town. In the middle distance the eye picks up the Roman arches of the railroad bridge, together with the belfry of Old Queens and some of the new high-rise Rutgers buildings on the far side; and the distant horizon closes in on the blue line of the Watchung Hills. This was the scene of action where Mabel Smith Douglass and her associates had their moment in history.

Douglass College, founded in 1918 as New Jersey College for Women, was a by-product of the larger movement for women's rights. Prominent among the forces that created it was the New Jersey State Federation of Women's Clubs. When the Federation leaders decided to promote a college for women resting on broad popular support, early in the second decade of the twentieth century, they met with varied response. From their own membership came enthusiastic approval. This was to be expected, for the feminist crusade was at high tide. The nation-wide General Federation of Women's Clubs had been in existence for twenty years, a more militant woman suffrage organization was active on a wide front, and the Nineteenth Amendment to the Federal Constitution was less than a decade away. Colleges for women were no longer a novelty, at any rate along the Atlantic seaboard. Vassar was preparing for its semicentennial; Elmira was even older. In the great state universities of the Middle West, and in many smaller private colleges as well, coeducation was firmly established.

But New Jersey was different. Statewide loyalty or support for any cause, not only the higher education of women, faced unusual obstacles, for the State lacked inner unity. Unlike its neighbors, New York and Pennsylvania, New Jersey had no central tradition or historically established character. Puritan influences existed, but it was never a

The Founding of the College

Puritan state like Massachusetts or Connecticut. There were Quakers, but they did not dominate as they had in early Pennsylvania. There were even, in colonial times, some slave-operated plantations, but New Jersey was not a planters' civilization like Virginia and the tidewater South. Dutch influence, once strong in the northern and central counties, was fading. And such unity as those various strains might have given the State was rapidly being dissipated by a flood of European immigrants into its industrial cities. Without an economic core, New Jersey was pulled in opposite directions by the two great metropolitan centers outside its borders, New York and Philadelphia. Thousands of Jerseyites, conducting their business or profession in one of these two cities, came home only to sleep. Their business connections, and consequently many of their civic and social interests, lay outside the State.

Education had always suffered from this bipolarity and general lack of unity. The growth of the public school system had been slow and sporadic, and New Jersey was one of the last states in the north to provide free, tax-supported schools for all its children. Higher education had fared better, but largely through private effort. Beyond authorizing an occasional lottery, the State had done little through the nineteenth century for its two leading colleges, Princeton and Rutgers. Besides, these two institutions were for men and, except for an occasional prophetic voice, were in no mood to depart from the all-male tradition inherited from their colonial founders. Princeton, it is true, had suffered a brief coeducational interlude in the form of a women's annex, known as Evelyn College, which flourished —or rather languished—for a few years in the eighteen-nineties. But the experiment ended when the enrollment

5

dropped to fourteen, and it was not revived.[1] A Roman Catholic institution for women, the College of St. Elizabeth, dating from 1899, served a limited clientele. But the State itself offered nothing.

Political equality for women, like educational opportunity, was late in coming. New Jersey, along with the Eastern states generally, refused women the vote. Following the example of New York, Pennsylvania, and Massachusetts, it rejected woman suffrage in a popular referendum as late as 1915. The only solace for the women of New Jersey was that the adverse vote—58 per cent—was smaller than in the other three states.

This was the State, these were the circumstances, in which a small group of leaders set out to build a college for women. The organization through which they worked and to which, in the long run, goes the chief credit for the founding of the college, was, as stated, the State Federation of Women's Clubs. Itself of recent origin and inexperienced in the tactics of joint effort for civic purposes, the Federation planned, agitated, collected funds, kept up the pressure and never let go until, after seven years, it had its college.

It all began when Mrs. Mabel Smith Douglass, a Barnard graduate and president of the College Club of Jersey City, was invited, late in 1911, to a district meeting of the State Federation of Women's Clubs.[2] At this meeting "the interest of the College Club was solicited in connection with the matter of opening Rutgers College in all its branches to the women of the State of New Jersey," [3] and Mrs. Douglass was persuaded to take the chairmanship of a Federation subcommittee to investigate possibilities. Never one to do things by halves, she threw herself into the project with those extraordinary powers of persuasion and leadership that she was to display so successfully in the years ahead. She familiarized herself with the origins and functions of institutions of higher learning in states comparable to New Jersey, and consulted their presidents and alumni. Through her Jersey City neighbor, James T. Fielder, who was at the time governor of New Jersey, she gained access to powerful political personages of state and nation, even securing an interview with President Woodrow Wilson. Rebuffed by philanthropic foundations to whom she had gone for large sums, she organized a popular one-dollar subscription fund for a first building, and spoke in support of it at countless meetings all over the state. She enlarged her committee to include an advisory council of prominent men and women, and with these preliminaries behind her, she approached the Trustees of Rutgers College.

Rutgers had been the choice of the Federation because Rutgers had become the land-grant college for New Jersey and received both federal and state funds, whose benefits, in the opinion of the campaign leaders, should in fairness extend to women as well as to men. A new private institution after the manner of the foremost Eastern colleges for women was not part of their thinking. For that matter, no Matthew Vassar or Sophia Smith had appeared in New Jersey to finance such a college. But public higher education for women had wide support. In the minds of many it was bracketed with other reform movements of this, the flood tide of the Progressive Era. A writer in the New Brunswick *Home News* envisioned the day when the men and women of New Jersey, sharing the suffrage, would make Rutgers the coeducational tuition-free state university, spreading enlightenment and culture "in a saloonless state." [4] Organized pressure groups rallied to the movement. The Granges fa-

The Rev. Dr. William H. S. Demarest,
President of Rutgers, 1902–1924

vored it; the militant feminists demanded it. A stiff little
note from the president of the Equal Suffrage League of
Summit to President Demarest of Rutgers makes their position perfectly clear: "My dear Sir: . . . We should like to
ask upon what grounds you justify the exclusion of women
from equal privileges with men in the Land Grant College
of New Jersey." [5] Rutgers, the publicly supported land-grant
college, thus seemed the logical place.

RESOLUTIONS
NEWARK, JUNE 10, 1914.

Whereas, there is no general opportunity for the young women
of the State of New Jersey to obtain a collegiate education within
the State, and

Whereas, it is believed by many that such opportunity should
be available to our young women similar to that open to the young
men of the State, and

Whereas, the New Jersey State Federation of Women's Clubs has
expressed itself in favor of a college for women affiliated with
Rutgers College:

Therefore, be it resolved; That we, the authorized committee
of the N. J. S. F. W. C. and its Advisory Council, inquire of the
Trustees of Rutgers College whether they approve the sentiments
hereinabove stated, and if so upon what conditions; and whether
they will direct the appointment of a committee to confer on the
matter with the committee of the N. J. S. F. W. C. and its Advisory
Council to the end that the need for the collegiate education of
women within our state may be the most speedily and effectively met.

But Rutgers was also a venerable independent college of colonial origins, and its long tradition of a classical education for young men only was not something to be lightly thrust aside. So President Demarest explained, courteously but firmly, to the feminists and all other interested parties. The Rutgers Trustees were in accord with the President and unwilling to remodel old Rutgers into a coeducational institution along western lines. The Trustees had rejected such proposals before. But they did show a cautious interest in a parallel, coordinate, women's college under the Rutgers charter, provided such an institution could raise its own funds and would not expect Rutgers to assume any financial obligations. Mixed apprehension and desire to seize new opportunities are reflected in their correspondence. "It has been impossible for me to take any definite attitude officially," the President confided to one member of the Board of Trustees. "And personally I have felt that I must not actively promote or discourage the movement. . . . If adequate funds were provided . . . Rutgers would welcome an affiliated Woman's College, but Rutgers could not assume any financial responsibility for it." And to another member: "I see no reason why we should set ourselves against the idea, yet I confess to a feeling of relief that no action is immediately impending." [6] For a little longer, old Rutgers would put off the plunge into a strange new world. In a similar vein, U.S. Senator—and Rutgers trustee—Joseph Frelinghuysen reported to President Demarest a first meeting with Mrs. Douglass: "As you say, she is reasonable and intelligent. . . . She wants $100,000. . . . I think the thing should not be turned down or ignored, as her inability to raise her fund will be a sufficient deterrent without any opposition on our part, and if it could succeed it would not be

James Neilson

Leonor F. Loree

so bad as it would not be a coeducational college but an affiliated college." [7]

But there was strong support, too, among the Trustees, from men like Drury W. Cooper and, above all, two who were to become the staunch supporters and benefactors of the young college through its first two decades, James Neilson and Leonor F. Loree. The Rutgers faculty, too, was generally favorable to the idea.

Mrs. Douglass, "reasonable and intelligent," sensed the equivocal climate. In a report to the Federation she warned: "This project must under no circumstances be called coeducation as that term would certainly draw forth opposition among the friends of Rutgers." A relationship like that of Barnard to Columbia seemed most desirable to her. And she went on to reassure Dr. Demarest: "As to coeducation—I would not worry about that—no one wants it—neither the parents of the girls nor the parents of the boys. The newspapers only have mentioned it and they more from the habit of being haphazard than anything else. I know that I would lose some of my best backers were I to propose coeducation." [8] Thus she allayed suspicion and gradually won the confidence of the Trustees to the point that, while urging the importance of adequate buildings and endowment, they expressed their willingness "to enter into affiliation with such a college if annual support of it be guaranteed to a satisfactory amount," and provided that it be located on land offered by Mr. Neilson, and that the faculty and the course of study be satisfactory. [9]

But then matters took an unfavorable turn. The drive for funds lagged, as Senator Frelinghuysen had foreseen, and the president of the Federation regretfully informed Rutgers that her organization had been unable to raise enough money

Drury W. Cooper, Rutgers Trustee and an early supporter of the College at the dedication in 1948 of a memorial plaque to Mrs. Cooper, also a founder and benefactor. Their daughter, Esther Cooper Poneck, was a member of the first graduating class

to erect a building and launch the college.[10] An even more damaging blow was the forced withdrawal of Mrs. Douglass from the enterprise. Worn down by overwork and domestic worries, she had been ordered by her physician to give up all her club activities and had left the state for an extended rest. Deprived of her leadership, the movement lost drive and direction. Other voices were heard, some suggesting a location closer to the population center of the state, perhaps in a suburb of Newark; still others urged the expansion of the Normal School at Trenton into a full college. The normal school movement had earlier given Mrs. Douglass some concern, and she had tried to head it off. "I scent something brewing in the Normal camp," she wrote Dr. Demarest. And again: "There is opposition in the Legislature from supporters of the Normal School. It is absolutely essential that we have [state] Senator Gaunt with us. Your Professor John Van Dyke is one who advocates a Teachers' College —do please lead him into the right paths." Her vision was larger. "What wouldn't I give to see New Jersey have a great state university, with the State Normal School, the woman's college, the graduate school and all located in one place and under one wise rulership!" [11]

With a reorganized committee, the Federation meanwhile continued to examine the various possibilities. Among other things, they arranged for a statewide survey by Professor Robert Scoon of Princeton University. The Scoon Report, in November, 1916, disclosed among other things that three-fourths of the state's school superintendents and high school principals believed that a college for women was urgently needed, that it should provide vocational training on a cultural basis, and that it should serve "girls who will be teachers or secretaries, and those who want a good general education plus training for efficient housekeepers." [12] As to location, the Report favored the Newark area. The new directions suggested by the Scoon Report, together with persistent rumors in Federation circles that Rutgers was not really interested, tended to weaken the entire drive and dissipate its momentum. It began to look as though the college, if it ever did come into existence, might not be affiliated with Rutgers at all.

But the protagonists of Rutgers did not remain idle. Prominent among them were Mrs. Adelaide Marvin, wife of Dean

Walter T. Marvin of Rutgers, and Mrs. Drury W. Cooper. A friend of Mrs. Douglass since their college days at Barnard, Mrs. Marvin was asked by Mrs. Douglass early in 1915 to take on some of her speaking engagements. In compliance, Mrs. Marvin spoke in fourteen New Jersey cities and towns in the next four months, and also before the annual convention of the Federation in Atlantic City in May. From her vantage point in Federation councils, she managed to keep the cause of Rutgers before the members, and also to keep President Demarest informed of new developments. Mrs. Cooper and others were instrumental in getting the New Brunswick Women's Club to raise a fund of over $5,000 and in inducing the city of New Brunswick to pledge $10,000 toward a college.[13]

Another supporter of affiliation with Rutgers was Elmer B. Boyd, owner of the New Brunswick daily paper, the *Home News*. This paper gave the movement full coverage in its news columns and carried sympathetic editorials. In one letter to President Demarest, Mr. Boyd confessed to "a great deal of interest in the plan to establish a New Jersey College for Women here," and called attention to the need for a tremendous effort if the college was to come to New Brunswick. Here, by the way, is one of the earliest instances of the use of what was to become the official name of the college: New Jersey College for Women. Mr. Neilson's generous property offer, Boyd thought, should be promptly accepted, and more money raised locally, lest the Federation place its college elsewhere. New Brunswick had missed out on a similar opportunity once before, over a century and a half earlier. When the newly-formed College of New Jersey—now Princeton University—was looking for a home, and the Trustees came to New Brunswick with a request for one thou-

The Carpender residence, later to become College Hall, in the nineteenth century

sand pounds New Jersey currency plus ten acres for a campus and two hundred acres of woodland for fuel, the town failed at the last moment to meet the full amount. The village of Princeton did, and the College settled there. Boyd went on to deplore the dearth of philanthropists in New Jersey; he also called Dr. Demarest's attention to an ugly rumor, "unkind and unfair," no doubt, that Rutgers was dragging its feet. In sum, "I certainly do not want to see New Brunswick and Rutgers lose that new institution that would mean so much to us both." [14]

With America's entry into the First World War in 1917 the college drive was slowed still further, as citizens, men and women alike, turned to war work. A college for women, at Rutgers or anywhere else in New Jersey, seemed more distant than ever. No one could have guessed that within

An early sewing class in the Home Economics Department, then housed in College Hall

a year a women's college as part of Rutgers would be an accomplished fact. Two things brought about this unexpected turn. In 1917, the Congress of the United States passed the Smith-Hughes Act, another in the series of legislative enactments supplementing and enlarging the original Morrill Act of 1862 which had created the state agricultural colleges throughout the nation. Among other things, this law appropriated funds for the teaching of home economics in all land-grant colleges. For New Jersey, this money went to Rutgers, which thus found itself in a position to finance at least one full four-year collegiate course for women, a teacher training course in home economics.[15] At about the same time, an attractive property bordering on the agricultural college campus in the outskirts of New Brunswick came into the market at a reasonable price. It was the John Neilson Carpender estate overlooking the Raritan river and including a large, solidly built, mid-nineteenth century brownstone residence.

The principal obstacles to the establishment of a college were thus suddenly removed. There were now available a campus, a building, and an assured income. But all this was to be had only on condition of affiliation with Rutgers. And now the Rutgers Trustees, whatever their previous hesitation, decided to act. They took a three-year lease on the Carpender property with an option to buy. (James Neilson made the eventual purchase possible.) Typical of the changing mood of the Trustees was the practical politician's comment of Senator Frelinghuysen, "It is better to have twenty thousand women with us and not against us." Under the prodding of Drury Cooper and James Neilson, they passed a resolution on April 12, 1918: ". . . that the Trustees of Rutgers College do establish a Woman's College as a department of the state university of New Jersey maintained by the Trustees." [16] In addition, the resolution laid down the general conditions under which the new institution was to function. Courses appropriate to the freshman year were to be offered the following September, and the faculty was to be made up of Rutgers professors plus such other instructors as might be secured. Financial maintenance was to be kept strictly separate from that of Rutgers. The state legislature was to be asked for financial support of the proposed college as a part of the state university similar to the College of Agriculture. A publicity campaign was to be launched in the State, if possible through the instrumentality of the Federation of Women's Clubs. Finally, a special committee was to draw up a course of study and to attend to other necessary first things, such as giving the institution a name.

The Founding of the College

Thus another American college was launched. Its beginnings, fragile and tenuous as they seem in retrospect, were not too different from those of hundreds of colleges that had preceded it. The new venture did not have the solid financial backing of some of the Eastern women's colleges, to say nothing of such recent institutions as Johns Hopkins, Stanford, or the University of Chicago. Yet it did enjoy—by virtue of its association with Rutgers—the prestige of a colonial charter, it had the moral if not the direct financial support of an established and reputable college, federal aid through the land-grant laws, and, uniquely in the history of American higher education, the enthusiastic support and continuing loyalty of a federation of women's clubs. These were assets not to be despised. And Mrs. Douglass made the most of them.

For it was Mrs. Douglass to whom the trustees entrusted the leadership of the enterprise. Restored in health and still intensely concerned, she was again available. Sorrow still attended her, for she had lost her husband, yet with characteristic courage and skill she had taken over the management of his business. President Demarest and those trustees who had met her earlier were agreed that she was the person to head the new college. In a letter of inquiry to Dean Virginia Gildersleeve of Barnard, Demarest had outlined the nature of the position as he conceived it. We want, he said, someone of "the finest personal quality, of high education, of tactfulness and business capacity." For so purely an administrative position advanced scholarly attainments seemed to him of secondary importance.[17] An enthusiastic reply from Dean Gildersleeve confirmed his judgment, and he wrote Mrs. Douglass on May 18, "It seems to me that you are the one we need as Dean of the Woman's College. Conference with my advisers sustains me in that. . . . The work is so important, such a splendid opportunity for high and far-reaching service, that I know it appeals to you and I hope that the way will be clear for you to accept it." She did accept, moved to New Brunswick early in the summer, and began to build her college.

*   *   *

The new institution was to be a coordinate college with a separate existence, largely autonomous, yet part of a larger whole. Though differing in detail, it belonged to a class of women's colleges already represented by Barnard, Radcliffe, and Pembroke, all three of which were related in some fashion to men's colleges or universities of colonial origin. The Rutgers trustees established it "as a department of the state university of New Jersey maintained by the Trustees." President Demarest thought of it as a department of the College of Agriculture, which was the channel whereby Rutgers qualified as the state university and the recipient of the Smith-Hughes funds.[18] It was not until 1930 that the State Board of Regents, created as a result of a survey of the relation of Rutgers to the State, recognized the women's division as an autonomous college within the University.

To call the affiliation with Rutgers a marriage of convenience would be to ignore the genuine good will and support for the arrangement which existed in the University, from the top echelons down. Once the die had been cast, both President Demarest and Dean Douglass supported the union and worked for its success with complete good faith. The same was true of many of the leading trustees. Others, probably a minority, remained skeptical and gave grudging consent. There must be some way, wrote one of the doubters, to keep the women's college as a separate activity, quarantined on a separate campus, and "though really run by Rutgers, as much as possible separated from Rutgers in the eyes of the public." [19] And so the young sister was received, with satisfaction by some, with apprehension by others, into what had heretofore been an all-male household. The achievement of complete *co*ordination in fact as well as in name was going to take time. The beginning was certainly marked by *sub*ordination. With the best intentions on the part of Rutgers, it could hardly have been otherwise. As it was, the Trustees consigned the new institution to the care of one small committee; the faculty—some of them —were willing to teach there in their spare time; and the Rutgers undergraduates approached the "coopsters," as the women students soon came to be called, with mingled condescension and pleasurable anticipation.[20] An early list of proposed new positions with attached salaries—probably for the guidance of the trustees' committee, ran as follows: One professor of English, $2,500 to $3,000; if a woman, $2,000 to $2,500; and mathematics, chemistry and other subjects followed, with the same discrimination. The faculty which Mrs. Douglass gradually assembled, especially the women members, found it difficult to gain equal status with their Rutgers colleagues and to be accepted as fully qualified university professors. Fifteen years after the opening it was still possible for a Rutgers administrator in charge of the summer session to venture the casual opinion that the faculty of the women's college was, by and large, not really of college caliber and unfit to teach in the Rutgers summer school —this though the particular department that gave rise to the administrator's observation happened at the time to be superior in advanced degrees, scholarly publication, and teaching experience to its Rutgers counterpart.

But there were advantages too. Prestige went with membership in a university, the larger title which Rutgers assumed in 1924. Students of the new college had access to the rapidly growing University Library, as well as to that on its own campus. The phenomenal growth both of the physical plant and the student body would have been impossible without repeated loans and subsidies from the parent body. Rutgers advanced the money still needed, after the generous gifts and concessions of Drury Cooper and James Neilson, to buy the two original buildings, the Carpender property already mentioned, and the Cooper residence, with acreage, across the street. The unique dormitory plan of

The original Cooper Hall

scores of small residences was realized through the credit of the University, amounting at times to more than a million dollars. Additions to the campus came as direct gifts of, or through favorable intervention by, trustees and other officials of the University, such as James Neilson, Leonor F. Loree, and Dean Jacob G. Lipman of the College of Agriculture.[21] On balance, it is fair to say that the College would have had great difficulty in surviving had it been forced to make its way alone, and not in affiliation with Rutgers University.

Not everybody in New Jersey was happy about the Rutgers connection. Some thought it a mistake to identify a project that had public, statewide support with an institution whose public status was still uncertain. Rutgers had not yet become unequivocally the state university, or completely shaken off the characteristics of a small, classical, private college, which it originally had been. Desire for an independent status for their college, more representative of the State as a whole, was widespread among the women's clubs. At a joint meeting of the Rutgers trustees' committee for the women's college with Federation leaders, on March 8, 1918, the chairman of the latter group expressed the hope that the new college might have its own trustees, choose its own faculty, set up its own curriculum. But when the decision for Rutgers was made a month later, the Federation accepted it and continued its support. Not so many others. A sizable segment of public opinion was reflected in the bitter criticism by a New Brunswick resident. "What New Jersey needs," he said, "is a real university of New Jersey, free for all, men and women alike. . . . The feeble and selfish and narrow effort at affixing a nominal annex to Rutgers College . . . was an unworthy, closeted attempt consigning to oblivion something deserving wide publicity . . . as a State undertaking detached from sectarian or private control." [22]

Aware of this undercurrent of dissatisfaction, Dean Douglass kept the public and statewide character of the College always in the foreground. From the beginning she had emphasized the State's responsibility for the education of its young women, and to the end of her administration she never left it out of sight. One might say that the women's college along with the agricultural college became the most "public" part of Rutgers University. This was reflected in the name of the new college. While various names had been suggested in the formative stages—Berkeley, Carteret, Queens, even Douglass by one prophetic soul—and while a Rutgers trustee derisively asked "Who would want to cheer for the Woman's College of New Jersey?," that is what it became. In view of the sources of support and the entire history of the movement, it had to be *New Jersey College for Women*.[23] This was soon abbreviated to N.J.C., and as N.J.C. it became affectionately known to thousands of alumnae.

What kind of college was it to be? In determining goals and planning a suitable course of study, the founders had two models before them. They might copy the leading women's colleges of the East and set up an academic curriculum modeled originally upon the old classical men's colleges, offering a full complement of languages, literature, science, and philosophy, with special attention to artistic and cultural values and only grudging concessions to practical and vocational needs. Or they might do the opposite and establish a purely vocational institution, designed to prepare its graduates for gainful employment as teachers, or dieticians, or secretaries in business and industry. As it turned out, the women's college in New Brunswick adopted neither plan in its entirety, but appropriated what it considered the best features of each.

The initial impetus was vocational, of that there can be no doubt. In the original appeal to the women—and men—of the state, the emphasis was on preparing New Jersey girls for useful and economically rewarding occupations at home, instead of having to send them out of the State or drawing in out-of-state residents for these positions. "Three hundred fifty-five college graduates were appointed in our public school system last year," said Mrs. Douglass early in the campaign, "all came from without the State. . . . Our greatest argument is to give the New Jersey girl a chance to compete with the girls of other states whose opportunities are so much greater." And in her first statement to the newspapers she again stressed the demand for college-trained girls as secretaries, court stenographers, teachers, and social workers.[24] The same point of view was evident in the first meeting of the Rutgers trustees' committee with the leaders of the Federation, when the chairman of the women's group insisted that the prime purpose of the College was occupational, that its course of study should be up to date and practical "and not have any old medieval fossil thrust upon it."[25] Even more compelling was the Smith-Hughes appropriation for home economics: a purely vocational grant which had made the opening of the College possible in the first place.

But other influences were at work as well. Many of the Federation leaders were, like Mrs. Douglass, graduates of liberal arts colleges. The whole weight of the Rutgers tradition was thrown on the side of the liberal arts, from President Demarest on down. He had made it clear from the outset that he preferred "oldfashioned college instruction in the fundamentals without any vocational training at all." [26] Dean Douglass' resentment at the rival attempt of the Normal School in Trenton to set itself up as the women's college of the state grew at least in part out of her conviction that a teacher-training institution was not the place to get a genuine college education. The Trenton type of vocational education, she wrote James Neilson, "is not what the young women of the state want nor is it what the Federation has been pleading for," but rather "a true *college* for women." [27] Not a scholar in the technical sense—the Barnard A.B. was her highest earned degree—Mrs. Douglass had a sound appreciation of cultural values, and throughout her fifteen years as Dean she resisted all attempts to emphasize the vocational at the expense of the liberal. In her introductory talk to the freshmen in September, 1931—the last she was to give—her theme was, as it had been many times before, the importance of being intellectually alive, of saturating oneself with literature, philosophy, and the social sciences, before deciding irrevocably on a career.

The influential Scoon Report of 1916 pointed the way toward a blending of the two ideals. The hundred high school principals and forty-three superintendents interviewed for this report almost without exception wanted a college which, while preparing teachers and secretaries and efficient homemakers, would offer a good general education and undergird all vocational courses with solid work in the humanities and sciences. This was what N.J.C. tried to do. The vocational interests, strong at the start, continued to maintain themselves, but the liberal academic features, under steady pressure from Dean and faculty, and with growing support from students and alumnae, grew steadily stronger.

The Founding of the College

In a radio talk near the end of her career Dean Douglass summed it up: While liberal and vocational courses, existing side by side, make for flexibility and open new vistas, "the duty of a college is primarily cultural." [28] And so, when classes began in September of 1918, the subjects of instruction were English composition and literature, Latin, Greek, French, and Spanish, history, chemistry, biology, mathematics—and on the vocational side, teacher education and, of course, home economics, the bread-and-butter course in more ways than one.

The management of the new college was entrusted to a committee of the Rutgers Board of Trustees. After two years, in 1920, the committee was augmented by the addition of four prominent members of the State Federation of Women's Clubs, appointed by the trustees, and was formally titled The Board of Managers of the College for Women. Enlarged a year later to six trustees and five Federation members, the Board continued in this form to the close of Dean Douglass' administration, in 1933. At that time it was renamed The Trustees' Committee on the College for Women, with the proviso that the Federation members be also elected trustees for their term of service, and that the current president of the Federation be an *ex officio* member. The duties of the board, as explained by President Demarest at their organizational meeting,[29] included the spending of all moneys, engaging the faculty and clerical help, taking charge of the property, establishing the curriculum, and generally directing policy, with all major decisions subject to review by the trustees of Rutgers.

From the beginning, the Board was a concerned and competent body of administrators. It regularly included some of the most prominent trustees, while the Federation posts were consistently filled by able and influential women. Relations with the State, meanwhile, were not neglected, and political fences were kept mended. Among the board members in those early years were a United States Senator from New Jersey, Joseph Frelinghuysen, and a member of the United States House of Representatives, Ernest R. Ackerman. It also included the vice-chairman of the Republican State Committee, Mrs. Lillian Feickert, who was asked to serve, as she herself said, "for my political affiliations and influence." [30] Such was the leadership that took the young college through its first perilous years.

~~~ 2

The Days of Dean Douglass

For the first fifteen years, New Jersey College for Women was the lengthened shadow of its Dean, Mabel Smith Douglass. A native of Jersey City, where she was born on February 11, 1877, Mabel Smith was of Dutch colonial stock, tracing her ancestry to the Reverend Evardus Bogardus, second Dutch Reformed minister in the American colonies. Her father died when she was very young, apparently leaving the family in comfortable circumstances. At any rate, books, music, and travel were part of her youthful environment. She remained all her life an omnivorous reader; she played the violin. After public elementary and high school in Jersey City, she went to Barnard College, graduating in 1899. In 1903 she married William Shipman Douglass, owner of a wholesale produce business. They had two children, both of whom were to die in tragic circumstances, the son in his teens, the daughter in her thirties. After the death of her husband in 1917 Mrs. Douglass managed his business for a year, then sold it when invited to become Dean of the College to whose founding she had contributed more than anyone else.

Like most successful administrators, Dean Douglass had a capacity for relevant labor. She put first things first and she was never far away from her job. During the entire first year she slept in her office: that was her home.[1] A page of scribbled entries chosen at random from her private memorandum book at that time speaks volumes. It includes a sketch of the first-year course of study, the telephone number of Senator Frelinghuysen, and two desperate entries: "find leak in coal bin," "fire escape—Dr. Demarest!!" There can be little doubt that conscientious attachment to her work, along with her personal tragedies, hastened her ill health and led to her comparatively early retirement and death.

The Dean's complete absorption in her College, her personal interest in its members and all its activities, shines through even such staid and starchy documents as her annual reports to the Board of Managers. Amid shortages and delays, "the students cooperated splendidly." Everything was fine, though the College was carrying on "in a private house, a made-over barn, a temporary gymnasium, and rented dormitories." Even a Hallowe'en party was worth reporting, in the Gymnasium, "which creaked and groaned under the strain." Buildings acquired or temporarily turned to new uses were "far from handsome" but "cleverly transformed" or "affectionately remembered." [2]

The Dean's powers of persuasion were phenomenal. She managed faculty and students with adroitness; she knew how to retain the loyalty and financial support of the women's clubs, and she lobbied competently in the State Legislature, which had not been in the habit of spending much money for higher education. Beginning with the second year and for almost a decade thereafter, she managed to secure increasing amounts for maintenance and appropriations for new buildings with almost automatic regularity. Her method was simple and thorough: she went to Trenton to see the key committee chairmen, took full advantage of her personal acquaintance with governors and legislators, and alerted the presidents of all the local women's clubs of the state to support her requests. In the light of such a record of success one can understand the insistence of the Board of Managers "that Dean Douglass, *in person*, plead the cause of the College for Women, as heretofore, before the State authorities." [3]

In all her dealings with men and affairs, Mrs. Douglass remained completely feminine. Though involved in the national movement for woman suffrage, of which her college was a by-product, she was not a militant feminist. Attractive and striking in appearance, with blue eyes and reddish-blond hair, she wore clothes well, set high standards of dress and conduct for all college affairs, and made students and faculty conscious of social proprieties. A student wearing dungarees or shorts in her day would have been blasted off the campus. There is a story, overdramatized perhaps but essentially true, that on her first visit to Mrs. Elizabeth Rodman Voorhees, donor of the Chapel, the Dean was induced to go in a severe tailored costume, quite out of character for her. The visit was not a success. She tried a second visit, and this time put on all her frills. The result was a million-dollar bequest. Rutgers administrators and professors, while by no means agreeing with all her views, were generally as ready to admit the power of her reasoning as of her personal appeal.

She used every opportunity to show off her College to the best advantage. Among other occasions, an evening concert dedicating the magnificent chapel organ gave her such an opportunity. It was of course a formal affair. Faculty members who attended—and all were expected to—told of being stopped at the door by the Dean, who looked them over and if she approved of their appearance, said, "You look nice, sit in one of the front pews." Any remonstrance that the professor preferred to sit elsewhere would have been held disloyal to the Dean and to the College.

With so much authority and responsibility, unhampered by precedent or tradition, Dean Douglass' regime took on a highly personal character. She chose her instructors and professors with considerable attention to personality factors, and while on the whole she assembled a capable and devoted faculty, not all her choices were wise. There were no regularities or gradations of salary or promotion, and tenure was unknown. Advancement came to those who, in the Dean's opinion, merited it. Without self-consciousness she habitually referred to "my students, my faculty, my college." Though consistently courteous, she did not like to be crossed and could be severe and sometimes arbitrary. The more extreme manifestations of personal government tended to disappear in her last years, when the growth of the institution and her own good sense led her to delegate responsibility and to work increasingly through and with others.

One of Dean Douglass' greatest contributions as an educator came in her relations with her students. In the early years, until the numbers grew too large, she knew them all by name, attended their social functions, danced with their escorts, interested herself in their lives, provided personal guidance and, when necessary, meted out discipline. Her chapel talks were informal and effective, though delivered in a high voice and with what was then known as a Jersey

The Days of Dean Douglass

City accent. She informed and explained, scolded and praised, as seemed necessary. Typical was her first talk to the freshmen in the fall of 1928.[4] It opened with some general phrases about the importance of combining a broad cultural education with specialized training, but soon got down to cases. To succeed in college, the Dean pointed out, you must be honest—first, last, and always. In freshman composition, write what you think, not what you think you ought to think. Dare to be simple, to be yourselves; don't ape those upperclassmen who think they are intellectual if they wear their hair slicked back and go to "ultra" plays, or those who think that to be progressive whatever is must be changed. Listening to inspiring class lectures is not enough; only those things will stick by you which you have painfully dug out for yourselves. If a professor is difficult and eccentric, think of your own idiosyncrasies and feel sorry for him, not for yourselves. The talk ended with a few consoling words on homesickness.

Another device for strengthening the bond with the students was her habit of taking student leaders into her confidence on matters of college policy. Treating them as adult equals when it suited her purpose, she told them of her toubles with the state legislature or the Rutgers Trustees and consequently lined them up solidly on her side in every controversy. In the historically valuable memoir of the class of '22, "In the Beginning," the author flatly states that the entire class assumed as a matter of course that Dean Douglass would accomplish anything she set out to do, and they were for it. In fact, the entire memoir, written thirty-five years after the event, is dominated by the towering figure of the first dean.

For all her versatility, Dean Douglass could not have succeeded in her undertaking without the unfailing support of several able administrative colleagues. There was Elisabeth N. Greene, who carried the title of Registrar but whose services and contributions extended far beyond her immediate professional duties. Alfred N. Henderson was an experienced financial official who managed the tenuous finances with tact and efficiency throughout the critical formative years. The sensitive task of providing student meals fell to Emma S. Jobbins, manager of Cooper Dining Hall to 1946.

A competent and devoted Board of Managers, made up of concerned Rutgers trustees and some of the ablest public-spirited women of the state, gave service far beyond the

Mrs. Wells P. Eagleton (l) and Mrs. A. Haines Lippincott (r), both of whom served more than twenty years on the Board of Managers and its successor, the Trustees Committee on the College for Women

call of duty. Three at least of these women must be mentioned here, for their years of courageous and intelligent leadership: Mrs. Wells P. Eagleton of Newark, Mrs. Edward J. Katzenbach of Princeton, and Mrs. A. Haines Lippincott of Camden. Active in the suffrage movement and, after the Nineteenth Amendment, in the League of Women Voters, or else in public education and progressive causes generally, these three women, through more than twenty years of service each on the trustees' committee, were a tremendous asset to the young College as it tried to find its place in the rapidly growing and changing state of New Jersey. The College has remembered them by naming dormitories after Mrs. Katzenbach and Mrs. Lippincott, while the Eagleton Institute of Politics is the memorial to Mrs. Eagleton.

Of the Rutgers trustees, two men stand out beyond all others: James Neilson and Leonor F. Loree. Without their continued moral and financial support the College might well have gone under. Both were Rutgers alumni who had been actively interested in their alma mater and now transferred this interest to the new sister institution. Mr. Neilson, grandson of a Revolutionary War veteran who had been chairman of the Rutgers Board of Trustees in the seventeen-eighties, gave large tracts of land to the College, which was almost literally growing up in his front yard. Antilles Field, Gibbons Campus, and white-pillared Wood Lawn, his ancestral home, with its surrounding acreage, all remain as visible evidence of his generosity. He took a personal interest in the students, invited them to his home for coffee and for evening dances, gave hotel dinners to graduating classes, gave financial support to the needy and used his influence in the State to find jobs for them after graduation. Pedagogical and moralizing harangues at student social functions gave him great pleasure. "Learn a bit about many things and much about at least one thing." (Here is the distribution-concentration principle of curriculum construction in a nutshell.) "Observe the laws of health." (He used to attribute his own longevity to eating raw cabbage, keeping a civil tongue in his head, and choosing his ancestors wisely.) "The frequent talk about leadership always amuses me. A leader may perhaps be made, but he must, I fancy, first be born; one can't really make a whistle out of a pig's tail." Then the ingratiating conclusion: "As an octogenarian I can confess frankly to love for you dear ladies who are making my old age happy." [5]

His interest in the students, who adored "Jimmy," their fairy godfather, occasionally brought him into conflict with the Dean, whom he otherwise ardently supported. He began asking for special privileges, which an impartial administrator could not in fairness grant. "I know," Mrs. Douglass wrote him on one occasion, "you have the best interests of the students at heart, but I am quite sure you cannot have any idea of the vast number of special privileges . . . which are being daily asked for. I could not possibly grant them and hope to hold the college together." [6] It was an understandable clash of two strong personalities devoted to the same cause. From then on, his annoyance at being thwarted led him to occasional sharp criticism of the Dean's "high-handed" methods. Yet when she retired in 1933, one of the finest and most genuine of the many letters of appreciation that poured in on her was from James Neilson. He remained a familiar figure on the streets of New Brunswick almost to his death in 1937, at the age of ninety-three.

While Neilson was the local patriarch, Leonor F. Loree was of national stature. Well-known railroad magnate, one of the last and most rugged of the nineteenth-century captains of industry, he was an imposing figure with an awe-inspiring beard. A shaker and a mover, when he gave orders things were done. When he invited the wife of the new President of Rutgers to inspect the N.J.C. buildings and campus, the latter by her own admission canceled all her engagements and meekly submitted to the guided tour. Though Loree made frequent visits of inspection to the campus, most meetings of the Board of Managers were held in his Wall Street office. When on rare occasions he did come out to New Brunswick for a meeting, College Hall prepared feverishly for the event. A new faculty member, unfamiliar with the ritual, breezed into College Hall one morning. Vaguely aware that the place was uncommonly subdued, he nevertheless blundered into various offices, exchanging pleasantries and not bothering to keep his voice down, until an imperious whisper from the head of the stairs stopped him in his tracks: "Shhh!! Mr. Loree is coming!" Mr. Loree was still a half-hour away, but the mood had to be created to receive him and levity was not in order.

The old railroad tycoon had a deep suspicion, like many a businessman before and since his day, that the average professor was inefficient and unbusinesslike. The faculty returned the suspicion and darkly hinted that Mr. Loree was about to install time clocks in all departments, that he wanted only one professor in each department, well-paid to be sure, to give all the lectures in a large classroom, supported by an adequate number of instructors reading student papers at clerks' wages. The faculty's suspicions were not unfounded, but Loree apparently never pressed his views to a conclusion with his fellow trustees.

Mr. Loree's intense interest in N.J.C. usually took a practical turn. He was the financial angel who came through in emergencies. Holes in the budget, inadequacies in the payroll, unexpected extras for which neither tuition funds nor the state appropriation sufficed—these were his concern. He arranged a gift of $50,000 to grade some land donated by James Neilson, provide it with a retaining wall and convert it into an athletic field. This was Antilles Field, named after the ship which had brought him and his family and friends back from Europe at the outbreak of war in 1914, became a troop transport after the entry of the United States, and was sunk by a German submarine. Time and again he met serious financial crises with his own gifts or with contributions solicited from his fellow magnates in Wall Street. The men from whom he extracted gifts of from $1,000 to $5,000 each included such industrial and financial giants as George F. Baker, Coleman DuPont, Eugene Grace, Edward S. Harkness (who canceled the mortgages on ten Gibbons campus houses), August Heckscher, Otto Kahn, Clarence Mackay, Ogden Mills, Thomas Fortune Ryan, and Gerard Swope.[7]

An early class in Physical Education

The Days of Dean Douglass

The drum and bugle corps as equipped by Mr. Loree

Whatever their motives, they all contributed to the survival of New Jersey College for Women.

Commencement speakers and musical talent for commencement programs were another of Loree's self-appointed tasks. The Gloria Trumpeters turned up at his instigation for nearly every festive occasion during the first ten years. Like James Neilson, he was a fanatic about student health; the two were mainly responsible for the four-year physical education requirement of the College's early years. He secured a regulation that students must attend all meals, with a neat little proviso that those who cut gym classes could not go to dances. He wanted the time from noon until three-thirty every day free from classes so that the students might be active outdoors; but the faculty did not cooperate.

Some of Loree's gifts bordered on the whimsical: equipment and uniforms for a drum and bugle corps, a snubbing post from the Delaware and Raritan Canal, the stone lions from in front of the old Waldorf-Astoria Hotel in New

York. The marching corps performed once, in red and white costumes, at the dedication of the first unit of Jameson Campus in 1928, then it died. There was a reason. Mrs. Douglass did not like it, but unwilling to challenge the great college benefactor openly on what was after all a minor issue, she worked through the students. "Spontaneous" letters appeared in *Campus News,* supported by editorials which, with due respect and gratitude to Mr. Loree, suggested that the marching corps smacked of garish sensationalism unworthy of college students.[8] As a result of this maneuver, tension increased between the Dean and her imperious trustee; but the drums and bugles were never heard again; they hung, mute and inglorious, in the recesses of the attic in Botany (now Biological Sciences) Building under the curious gaze of freshmen and sophomores as they climbed up there for their history classes. The stone lions rested in their crates behind Cooper Hall for months, then miraculously disappeared. Another Loree gift, a bronze figure of a World War I Red Cross nurse at the edge of Antilles Field, was similarly misunderstood. Later generations of students, ignorant of its history and phonetically calling the athletic grounds Aunt Tillie's Field, naturally assumed that the bronze lady was Aunt Tillie. She was melted down for scrap in World War II, serving her country to the last.

*   *   *

The most pressing need confronting the Board of Managers in those early years was an adequate physical plant. Two old residences, no matter how stoutly built, did not suffice for an infant college of such lusty growth. Rutgers had done much but could not be expected to underwrite current expenses. A separate fiscal office was therefore set up with a bursar in charge. From this time, too, requests for legislative appropriations for maintenance as well as capital expenditures were kept separate, like those of the College of Agriculture, from the general university budget. Prime mover of all this was once again Mr. Loree, but he had the hearty approval of President Demarest.[9] Thus for the women's college, the separate line-item budget, whose merits were to be much debated in later years, was established with the full consent, if not at the instigation, of the parent institution.

The first year's financial report was not encouraging: $38,012.83 had been spent, against an income of $29,791.08. No margin for growth there. Yet within the next twelve years the miracle had happened; and before Dean Douglass retired, the physical plant, the buildings that made up N.J.C. as its graduates were to remember it for the next thirty years, had taken shape. For a quarter-century thereafter, from about 1930 to 1955, no substantial additions were made except the Student Center in 1953; then came the second wave of expansion, which resulted from the final transformation of Rutgers into the State University and produced the College that the students of its fifth decade were to know.

The details of that first expansion were as follows: Classroom space was presently provided by the State. Successive annual appropriations made possible the erection of the three main classroom buildings: Science, Recitation, and Botany, which were opened in 1924, 1926, and 1927 respectively. The origin of these three rather inappropriate names, so familiar to generations of students, remains uncertain. "Science" was perhaps the least objectionable, for the building did house the Chemistry Department and the Home Economics establishment with the experimental cafeteria. Yet

Botany laboratory in the early 'twenties. The young instructor is Miss Jessie Fiske

classes in the humanities edged in too, and the large hall on
the ground floor became the campus home of the commuting
students, the Bees. While Botany did contain the botany
office and a laboratory, it was also the headquarters of history
and the social sciences, and for a time of modern languages.
Most unsuitable as a name for a college building was Recitation, with its grammar school overtones. Two of its floors
were given over almost entirely to the college library, which
remained there until the opening of the new library building
in 1961; for the rest, the English Department had its home in
Recitation for many years, the Art Department occupied an
office, a lecture room and a studio, and language and mathematics classes met there too. In 1965 the three buildings were

appropriately renamed Chemistry, Biological Sciences, and Arts.

Oddly enough, these three buildings, instead of being grouped about College Hall or otherwise symmetrically arranged, were pushed off to one edge of the campus. A local situation was responsible. In the middle nineteen-twenties the State Highway Commission was planning a new road (the present U.S. Route 1) and tentatively routing it through New Brunswick. Rumor had it that the road was to come down Jones Avenue, shear off the north end of the campus and exit over a new bridge somewhere near the foot of Bishop Street. To forestall this mutilation, the Board of

Recitation Hall, one of three classroom buildings provided by the State in the College's first decade. It was renamed Arts Building in 1965

43

Federation Hall, a gift of the New Jersey State Federation of Women's Clubs, housed zoology and botany laboratories until 1960, when it became the Admissions Office

Managers, at the instigation of the Messrs. Loree and Neilson, had these three buildings placed at the far north end of the campus, squarely across the path of the proposed state highway.[10]

The State of New Jersey had met immediate needs, but for anything beyond that the College had to look elsewhere. Once again the State Federation of Women's Clubs stepped in. Their first contribution had been a science building in 1922, appropriately named Federation Hall, which housed zoology and botany laboratories and collections. This was followed by their major effort, the Music Building. In a statewide campaign—103 local clubs were listed in the dedication program in 1928—about $100,000 was raised for its erection. Though the total cost of the building, higher than estimated, went somewhat beyond this figure, the stately

Georgian structure on Sonomon's Hill, well suited to its purpose, remained a monument to the Federation and a reminder of its unique role as the only state federation of women's clubs in the nation to have led a movement resulting in the founding of a college.

The largest single gift during that first decade produced the most distinctive building: the Chapel. Focus of the sprawl-

Elizabeth Rodman Voorhees Chapel

ing campus, this structure in the Christopher Wren tradition with its white spire first catches the eye, whatever the direction of approach. It was made possible by the very generous bequest of Mrs. Elizabeth Rodman Voorhees, which sufficed not only for the building itself with its pipe organ, but for maintenance, broadly conceived, and for the enrichment of the entire music program. Worship services, choir concerts and musical programs of all kinds, commencement exercises, as well as student assemblies and public lectures, soon found their way into this multipurpose building.

An important and enjoyable addition to the educational program and the cultural life was the Dramatic Arts Building on Nichol Avenue, completed in 1926. Popularly known as the Little Theater, its original purpose was indicated by Dean Douglass, who, when reporting its completion, referred to it as "the building for spoken English." [11] This purpose was never lost sight of: proper voice production

The original gymnasium, built of World War I surplus packing boxes

Members of the class of 1923, housed temporarily in "packing box" gymnasium in 1920

and clear articulation were not only emphasized in the required speech classes, but added distinction to the plays, averaging three a year, with which the Department of Speech and Dramatic Art delighted students and townspeople alike.

Two more useful buildings, both landmarks of the nineteen-twenties, deserve notice. They are the Gymnasium and Cooper Hall. Hardly worthy of mention in the same breath with the stately Music Building and the noble Chapel, they nevertheless figured prominently in the daily life of the campus and are held in affectionate, or rueful, remembrance by thousands of alumnae. The story of the Gymnasium has often been told. A "temporary" structure, built of World War I surplus boxes in which airplane engines were to have been shipped to Europe, it was briefly used as a dormitory. Then it housed the entire indoor physical education program for the next forty-three years and continued in use even after the first unit of the Loree Gymnasium was opened in

47

January of 1963. Before the erection of the Chapel, daily assemblies and Sunday vespers were held in the Gymnasium too, as well as concerts, plays, and dances. As for Cooper, the residence on George Street secured from the Drury W. Cooper family, it was, in the words of the Dean, "at best a temporary structure and far from handsome," but it could be altered and expanded at comparatively little cost and thus lent itself to sudden and unpredictable needs. Patch by patch, as necessity dictated, this old Victorian house rambled down George Street until it reached Nichol, turned up Nichol to Redmond, and doubled back on itself. Inside, it was a maze of dining halls and kitchens. At various times it also contained committee rooms and offices, the infirmary, student and faculty lounges, and living quarters for members of the college family.

Strange things happened in Cooper, and not only to students. On one occasion the President of the University,

The first infirmary in Cooper Hall

48

scheduled to preside at a formal dinner in the upstairs banquet hall, blundered in by the wrong door, lost his way and fetched up in the boiler room. There he encountered the frightened wife of a new faculty member, equally lost; they joined forces and together battled their way to daylight and dinner. At another time a professor who had her living quarters in Cooper was caught for hours with her luggage in the freight elevator, which had broken down between floors. It was the first day of vacation and the building was already emptied of all occupants. By chance, the manager of the dining hall decided on a final tour of inspection, heard the calling and pounding, freed the prisoner and averted tragedy.

But the great need was for dormitories. With the enrollment exploding from fifty-four to 1,023 in ten years, every effort had to be made to provide living quarters for students. After various unsatisfactory makeshifts, the trustees' committee settled on the small-house plan—a group of residences, each designed for twelve to twenty students and arranged in a semicircle around a central recreation or common purpose building. These groups of homes became a distinctive feature of the campus and set N.J.C. living arrangements apart from those of most other colleges. The original idea apparently was the Dean's, who "thought of and investigated" the plan as a practical way of financing a dormitory building program. Mortgage money was available, which in her thinking would in time be amortized by student rentals. When clear of encumbrances, the houses could be leased to faculty or sold to private owners, provided the college had meanwhile erected large dormitories of the conventional type.[12]

The first twelve houses were built in 1922 on land newly acquired in upper Nichol Avenue; seventeen were added in the next three years, all of them together constituting a double horseshoe, with the Lodge, a recreation building, as the focus of one, and the Little Theater of the other. Tennis courts occupied the central space; an old mulberry tree was left standing between two courts, and when the ripe fruit fell the game took on a gory character. At the request of the students, the new community was named Douglass Campus. In 1926 a similar group of houses was begun on land above the Raritan donated by Mr. Neilson; twenty-two houses were eventually built there, also grouped around a recreation building, the Cabin. At Neilson's suggestion it was named Gibbons Campus.[13]

The small-house plan proved so satisfactory that what had started as a makeshift became standard practice. The author-

Dormitory room in Cooper Hall about 1923

Gibbons Campus in the late 'twenties

ities gave up all thought of disposing of the small residences and, instead, built the campus life around them. Four decades later they were still occupied by a large percentage of the student body. The Dean completely changed her mind about their temporary character and said, in 1928: "The large dormitory associated with so many American colleges probably will never be built here." [14] In this she was mistaken, for the very next dormitory built was of the conventional type: a series of red brick Georgian buildings arranged in a quadrangle of which only three sides were completed. Most of the land for this campus was acquired through the generosity of a Rutgers trustee, Edwin M. Jameson, and was named in honor of his wife, the Mary Gardner Jameson Campus. In addition to living quarters, this campus contained the infirmary, a recreation lounge [Calumet], an assembly room [Agora], and a swimming pool.

51

Students in a living room in Jameson Campus, first units of which opened in 1928

Begun in 1928, the last unit of Jameson was completed in 1931. With it, the first building program came to an end. Twenty-two years were to elapse, years of depression, war, and uncertain state relations, before the College acquired another new building.

* * *

On December 13th, 1918, the faculty of New Jersey College for Women met for the first time in formal session, to organize the academic program, plan procedures, make rules, and set precedents. President Demarest opened the meeting with prayer—no precedent was set here—and then yielded the chair to Dean Douglass. The entire faculty was present. It included eleven professors from Rutgers led by Dean Louis Bevier, and five members appointed to the women's college alone.[15] Beginning with these sixteen, the faculty increased rapidly in size over the years, keeping pace with expanding enrollments, and each year the proportion of Rutgers professors declined. In 1927, when the total faculty had grown to eighty, forty-seven were full-time N.J.C. members, and thirty-three were Rutgers men serving part-time. After another five years only three of the latter were left, and only one department still had a Rutgers man as head. Dean Douglass deliberately encouraged this trend toward autonomy, though she fully appreciated the importance of having experienced professors on hand at the outset to establish academic standards and set the intellectual tone. But Rutgers professors were not always available to meet sudden curricular needs; besides, morale could be built and unity of purpose best promoted by a faculty whose major commitment and loyalty were to the new college and not to the parent institution across town. Mrs. Douglass held consistently to this view and urged it on the trustees' committee time and again. Having repeatedly pointed out that the College was accumulating too many young, inexperienced, or part-time instructors, she was finally authorized in 1927 to enlarge the faculty by a number of experienced persons who were to come with professorial rank: two each in the classics, English, physical education, and Romance languages, and one each in botany, economics, education, history, and mathematics, at salaries up to $5,000.[16] This marked the turning point; hereafter, the allegiance of the faculty was to N.J.C. first, and then to Rutgers.

Salaries in those early years were uneven and capricious. A uniform salary scale for the whole University, with maximum and minimum levels for each rank and regular increments, was still decades in the future. Within the limits of the budget the Dean hired men and women who pleased her at salaries that varied considerably, and gave increases to those who in her opinion deserved them. In 1924 the salary scale ranged from $1,600 to $6,000. The Dean and the Bursar received the top figure. The highest-paid professor—a man—received $3,600, the highest-paid woman $2,400. There was some correction of this imbalance when a number of women of professorial rank arrived after 1927.[17]

Salary differentials failed to spoil the generally pleasant relations between the Dean and the faculty. Mrs. Douglass had the loyalty of her colleagues. Few opposed her, not only because this could prove uncomfortable—she was capable of drill-sergeant tactics in dressing down a recalcitrant instructor—but because there was little disposition to disagree with her policies. Barring a handful of critics, faculty opinion ranged from rational approval of her administration to open enthusiasm for her leadership. The feeling held even when she corralled them to vote as a bloc in University faculty meetings against measures that displeased her.

With the immediate needs of her College uppermost in her mind, Dean Douglass was not at all anxious to have her faculty take part in graduate instruction, which was coming to life in the University, nor was she interested in scholarly research as such. Had she believed that research and publication would raise the prestige of N.J.C., she would no doubt have encouraged it. The Trustees supported this view and affirmed that the college for women was not concerned with graduate instruction. Only by special permission might the faculty take on graduate courses, and then only "provided the undergraduate work at N.J.C. does not suffer."[18] This policy, understandable for the formative years when the young institution was trying to achieve identity, remained in force long after Dean Douglass' day, with not altogether happy consequences for the faculty. It placed them in an invidious position in later years, when the graduate program grew in size and importance and promotion and tenure in the university were increasingly based on productive research.

The course of study for which the faculty assumed responsibility in that December meeting in 1918 contained little that was new or startling. Ancient and modern languages and literature, mathematics, laboratory science, history—it was essentially the freshman program of Rutgers or, for that matter, of most American colleges of that day. The novelties were home economics and, a little later, music and painting. Three degrees were to be awarded: the A.B. for those who concentrated on Latin and Greek, the Litt.B. for those emphasizing modern languages, and the B.Sc. for those with a primary interest in science or home economics. This too was conventional college practice. To enter the A.B. curriculum, a girl had to offer four years of high school Latin or three years of Greek. Today, such a requirement would be incredible, yet the faculty of 1918 voted it without batting an eyelash. And many students qualified.

It was a program that honored tradition without ignoring practical needs; it was the pragmatic approach which has characterized the College from that day to this. Douglass College has never allowed itself to be drawn into controversies over the real purpose of women's colleges, at least not to the extent of taking an absolute position. It has never maintained, on the one hand, that every subject in the curriculum must justify itself as in some special way necessary and proper for women *qua* women; nor has it on the other hand regarded its students as sexless intellectuals and belligerently insisted on feeding them the same curriculum, no more and no less, that was offered in colleges for men. Its unspoken motto has been: let us do the one and not neglect the other. It has always stood for the supremacy of the trained intellect, ethically motivated and socially responsible; at the same time it has always maintained courses and programs of special concern to women, without shouting *Vive la différence.*

As numbers grew and classes were added, the simple course of studies of the first years was rapidly enlarged and diversified. The seventeen subjects and thirty-four full year courses offered in 1919–1920 had grown to twenty-seven and 181, respectively, ten years later.[19] In the beginning it was not uncommon for courses to be set up to meet student requests from year to year, without much attention to prerequisites, sequences, or standard requirements. The Dean approved, for she preferred to "fit the college to the students,"[20] not *vice versa.* Had she had a free hand, she might well have fashioned a college like Sarah Lawrence or Bennington. But rapid growth, as well as the association with Rutgers and the State, made such free-wheeling innovations unrealistic; in the circumstances, eventual conformity and standardization were inevitable.

Equipment and teaching aids were primitive. The sciences got the lion's share of the meager funds. They needed more, of course; then, too, the first full-time staff member of professorial rank not borrowed from Rutgers was a scientist, and he wielded considerable influence. Physical education was also firmly established. All students were required to take it all four years: Messrs. Loree and Neilson had seen to that. In the distribution of departmental funds for 1922–1923, for example, home economics was given $3,000, bacteriology $2,000, chemistry $1,500, botany, physiology, and physics $1,000 each, and hygiene $500. On the other hand, Romance languages had to get along with $100 and history with $50; Latin, Greek, and English got nothing at all. In later years, to be sure, these extreme discrepancies were partially rectified.

The library was nonexistent: there were no books and no building to house them. Mrs. Rosamond Sawyer Moxon '29, in her sparkling twenty-fifth anniversary sketch, puts it bluntly:

In 1918 all of the N.J.C. library, consisting of about a dozen books sent over from Rutgers, was in College Hall on the desk of the registrar, who kept the record of loans on a slip of paper. From her desk the library expanded to a shelf, thence to a locked closet in the middle room. Library hours, of course, were confined to those when there was someone around to unlock the door. Later the closet was left unlocked and the girls kept the record of books borrowed on a card in the closet.[21]

As long as such conditions prevailed, instruction in literature, history, and all the liberal arts was bound to be inadequate, even though the courses were taught by able professors, including some of the foremost members of the Rutgers faculty.

At its first meeting, the faculty plunged into routine housekeeping chores from which it has never emerged. Agenda and discussions were soon rumbling along in the familiar grooves of course descriptions and schedules, grading systems, class attendance regulations, and all the rest of the mechanics of academe, which no conscientious faculty can avoid. And like faculties everywhere, it occasionally allowed pedagogy to degenerate into pedantry, when in the heat of debate educational principles which seemed clear enough in the abstract were blurred with casuistry. The

The first library, housed in College Hall, now part of the Registrar's office

following bits, picked at random from the faculty minutes of the first decade, will give the flavor. To one who has never dealt with college problems, some of them will seem picayune and incomprehensible; the hardened professional will find them familiar and perhaps necessary.

There was the inevitable committee to determine the reason for so many failing grades. Another dealt with the mathematics and ethics of class attendance: how many tardinesses were equal to one absence? Were three class cuts as grave an offense as one chapel cut? How long should a class wait for a tardy instructor? Twenty minutes was thought to be about right, for a professor might be delayed coming across town from his last Rutgers class. Could individual professors be trusted to decide how much weight to give to the final examination in determining semester grades, or should this be done by collective action of the faculty?

Sundry other regulations were as follows: In establishing the ritual for graduation, the faculty resolved to march in direct order of rank at commencement, but to reverse the order for the baccalaureate service. (In later years, when space was at a premium, the faculty procession was abandoned.) A formal resolution changed the name of the Department of Physical Education and Hygiene to the Department of Hygiene and Physical Education. A member of the first graduating class had failed the second semester of American history in her senior year. It was resolved that she be given a reexamination; if she failed again, a course in the history of education which she had passed was to be accepted as a substitute, but she was not to be told of this in advance. The student passed the reexamination, graduated with her class, and has since distinguished herself in alumnae and civic affairs.

When growing numbers made the Dean's personal government less viable, faculty responsibilities broadened. Committees multiplied as the Dean shared more of her authority with her colleagues. Meetings became regular and frequent, and long-term planning took up more and more of the faculty's time. Departmental honors programs of individual study were introduced, beginning with the English Department in 1927. Relations with students and student organizations were regularized. As new needs arose, the faculty began to depart from the practices of the parent institution and came to exercise more complete control over the departments of instruction than was the habit at Rutgers, where departments enjoyed considerable autonomy. The faculty even took an occasional look at the world beyond the campus gates, as when it approved the Briand-Kellogg Pact in 1927 and informed the two senators from New Jersey of its stand.[22] In general, the late 'twenties were a time of tightening academic standards and improved intellectual tone; as Dean Douglass' regime drew to a close, she and her faculty had achieved an efficient and harmonious undergraduate college for women.

But faculty and administration could not have done it alone. The students contributed their share, a share that was greater in those formative years than at any time since. It was then that creative imagination was called for. The faculty, while often forced to innovate and improvise, did have Rutgers precedents to guide them; the fifty-four girls who matriculated at the new college in September of 1918 had none, except for the ready-made curriculum and the $100 tuition fee, both taken from Rutgers. In addition they paid $45 in fees and $320 for board and room. Within this framework, the college was theirs to make.

The college year had hardly begun when a blow struck that almost wrecked the institution before it could get started. This was the autumn of the "Spanish" influenza, and it hit the campus two weeks after the opening of classes. In the crowded dormitories contagion was inevitable, and nineteen students and two instructors were soon down with the disease. Doctors were overworked, nurses unavailable, and there was nothing to do but declare a recess and send the girls home. To add to the discouragement, the terrific ammunition explosion at Morgan on Raritan Bay occurred about this time and led timid folks to the conclusion that life in and about New Brunswick was not safe. Many thought this was the end; yet after three weeks, when classes resumed, all but four of the freshmen returned. Meanwhile, the Dean herself had been felled by a severe attack of influenza, and in her absence Alice Aronoff, instructor in physical educa-

tion, and Elisabeth N. Greene (now Mrs. Moncure C. Carpender), Registrar and Bursar, kept things going. Spirits
were still low, however, and the Registrar decided that a
diversion, something gay, was needed to restore morale. So
she arranged a formal dance with the cooperation of President Demarest. Any lingering doubts of the full support of
Rutgers for the new enterprise must surely have been dis-
pelled at the sight of the saintly Dr. Demarest, valiantly
holding up his end of the receiving line at a student dance.[23]

Another glimpse of that first winter comes from Dean
Douglass' *Personal Recollections*.[24] In order to secure the
first legislative appropriation she had, typically, alerted "the
Federation, Mothers' Congress, the D.R.'s, the D.A.R.'s, the
Suffrage and the Anti-Suffrage, the Colonial Dames, the
W.C.T.U.'s, and women members of boards of education.
Together we went to Trenton . . ." Their lobbying resulted
in a visit by a legislative committee. "The day the legislators arrived in New Brunswick was bitterly cold. . . .
The men entered College Hall to find classes dismissed, the
furnace being old and totally inadequate. After visiting the
offices and classrooms, the investigators went upstairs, and
there discovered the young women studying in coats and
galoshes, huddled around little coal stoves or small oil heat-
ers, for on the third floor there was no other form of heat.
But all were smiling, cheerful, and welcoming the visitors
from Trenton, told them that they loved the college and
would not be anywhere else." The end result was a $50,000
appropriation, the first of many, and it put the College on its
feet.

In the three years which followed that first arduous winter
the class of '22 set precedents, initiated traditions, and established the character of N.J.C. They adopted a college

motto and designed the college seal.[25] Apparently there was enough knowledge of the classical languages to permit an intelligent choice among the various Greek and Latin epigrams submitted. A member of the class wrote the words and music of the Marching Song as well as the text of the original Alma Mater.[26] Music for the latter was composed by Howard McKinney, professor of music at Rutgers; its official status ended in 1955, when the college changed its name and the topical contents of the text were thought no longer relevant. The old Alma Mater was difficult to sing, with its dreamy waltz tune that changed in midstream to a brisk march tempo, yet it was original and specific both in text and music—a rare occurrence among American college songs, which run to bland generalities and borrowed tunes.

The class of '22, as well as succeeding classes in the 'twenties, raised astonishing amounts from sales and auctions. A flower and rummage sale in 1926 yielded $3,204.10.[27] The money thus collected was not always spent, but sometimes dedicated to a future need, and occasionally funds deposited in some bank of the State for such a purpose were lost sight of as the classes that had raised the money graduated. In 1948, a bank in Jersey City inquired of the Physical Education Department what it intended to do with the money deposited to its credit in 1928. The Department knew nothing of this balance, but research showed it to have been the return from one of these auctions. With accumulated interest, it proved enough to build three hard-surface tennis courts.[28]

The first graduating class founded clubs and organizations of which many have lasted to this day. The handbook for information (the *Red Book*) for 1922 listed the following: the Undergraduate Association, the Bees, Choir, Glee

The members of the Class of 1922 dance about the May
pole on Mothers' Day

Club, Mimes, Pen and Brush, Philolethean, Scissor-bowl
(for home economics students), Social Service Club,
Y.W.C.A.—all names that most alumnae will recognize. The
first handbook also mentioned Campus Night, Christmas
Dance, Mothers' Day, Yule Log, and that "oldest custom:
no student shall be seen off campus without a hat." This last,
according to the handbook, had won the admiration of the
townspeople. The new college was on trial and had to make
good in the eyes of New Brunswick and New Jersey. Also
contributing to the respect of the townspeople was the directive that sophomores take freshmen to church on Sundays.
This may have been the outgrowth of a formal request by
President Demarest "that the students of New Jersey College for Women do not attend the Sunday morning services
at Rutgers College Chapel." [29] Whether lack of seating space

Class costumes in 1926

The Christmas ceremony, held in College Hall before the
Chapel was built

or some other dark reason prompted this request was not made clear.

The expanding *Red Book* reflected the growth of the institution. With increasing numbers, the improvisations and casual customs of the early years perforce hardened into fixed rules and standard procedures, with a corresponding loss of flexibility. Yet a surprising degree of spontaneity remained. N.J.C. retained a youthful freshness; it never degenerated into a bureaucratic machine or an assembly-line college. Chief among the factors that contributed to this happy result was the type of student government that was devised and hammered out over the years by cooperative effort.

The undergraduate association mentioned in the *Red Book* for 1922 was enlarged two years later into the Cooperative System of College Government, provided with a

Drama group from the first class in James Barrie's *Quality Street*, 1919

constitution and approved by the faculty.[30] This form of government, though renamed and revised many times over since its beginning, has remained the basic principle in the organization of the college. The key word is "cooperative." Perhaps a better word would be all-inclusive, for the entire College community, administration, faculty, and students, participated to a degree commensurate with the authority vested in each by the Trustees and the university charter. No one, from the Dean to the lowliest freshman, was left out. No one could be deprived of his constitutional rights, nor could any one, faculty or student, disaffiliate or disavow a share of responsibility for the good of the whole. The system was not static but in continuous evolution. When channels of communication clogged up, they had to be reopened; regulations that had grown obsolete had to be changed; new situations demanded new measures or new machinery. The government association was under constant criticism, no one was ever completely satisfied with it. That was why it continued to function.

Indispensable for the success of the system was the assumption of collective responsibility by the students for the integrity of their academic and social life: the honor system. This too evolved by trial and error. Though enthusiastically approved by the students at the outset, its novelty and its high demands on the individual presented difficulties as soon as actual cases of violation arose; besides, a minority of students remained unsympathetic to the principle itself. In 1927 and 1928, the critical years, the faculty minutes record twenty-eight disciplinary recommendations from the student judicial board, every one of which was approved. Penalties for major offenses ranged from two weeks' suspension to outright expulsion. The most lurid case in these years was that of a girl charged with "lying, drinking, smoking, un-chaperoned automobiling, late return, and false registration." She had pretty well exhausted the calendar of crimes and they threw her out. This one cleared the air; the determined stand of administration, faculty, and students decided the issue. From this time on the honor system was accepted as an integral part of the educational experience at N.J.C. By way of underlining the common purpose, the faculty passed a resolution of thanks to the student judicial board and its chairman for the year's work.[31]

A student newspaper, that standard feature of American campuses, appeared in November, 1920. Known as *Campus Chatter* in its first incarnation, it was printed on coarse paper, of tabloid size, and came out once a month for six issues. It recorded social events, club meetings, and box scores of basketball games; it carried some verse, short impressionistic sketches by students, and jaded he-and-she academic jokes: "Do you like caviar?" "I never took his course."

A year later the name was changed to *Campus News*, which lasted to 1940. Now on a better quality of newsprint, the paper grew in size and scope and became a varied and often lively journal. Social activities still furnished a large part of the grist. Glee club concerts, class banquets, Soph Hop, Junior Prom, Campus Night filled the columns. "Der Deutscher Verin Dance" proclaimed a headline the composer of which was obviously not a German major. Letters to the editor, the usual mixed bag, might commend the new government association or disapprove the wearing of earrings in class as "the height of poor taste." But intellectual activities were not neglected. Book reviews appeared regularly. One, on Sinclair Lewis' *Babbitt*, ended with the confession: he might be almost any one of us. Debates were reported, ranging from the problem of world disarmament to the ethics of bobbed hair. In those days, N.J.C. engaged in intercollegiate debates, a wholesome discipline which latter-day Douglass students were apparently no longer willing to undergo. Among their opponents were Bucknell, the women's team from Syracuse, and Rutgers. *Campus News* reported at length on papers read at club meetings, on topics such as the French occupation of the Ruhr, and an illustrated series on life in European universities.

Editorials were didactic and "nice." They approved flower day, physical activity, self-improvement, and free speech in the abstract. They commented on student government (it is probably a good thing if we are ready for it), on final examinations (they are rough but good for you). There was a desire to please, the editors wanted to see eye-to-eye with the authorities; no deep cleavages were apparent between students and faculty, and of militant crusading there was not a trace. Nor was there any evidence of the flapper, the revolt of youth, or the lost generation, all of which presumably characterized the nineteen-twenties. In the next decade the paper was not to be so docile.[32]

When the time came for the class of '22 to graduate, its members expressed the ardent wish to have their own commencement on their own campus. The Trustees agreed, "after thoughtful consideration," and the class had set a precedent.[33] In keeping with all academic tradition, a baccalaureate service was held in St. John's Episcopal Church on George Street—there was as yet no chapel. The rector of the church, the Rev. Edward W. Hall, was in charge of the service. Commencement in the packing-box gymnasium

Dean Douglass and Dr. Demarest lead the academic
procession at the 1924 commencement

was on Saturday, June 10. The Gloria Trumpeters furnished music; a Phi Beta Kappa section of the Rutgers chapter was instituted by Oscar Voorhees, national secretary of the Society, an unusual honor for so young a college; a senior orator spoke on "The Creative Instinct" and the chief commencement speaker, Agnes Repplier, on "The Failure of Success," Dean Douglass presided, and President Demarest offered the invocation and the benediction and gave out the diplomas.

Commencements were not the only festive occasions in the nineteen-twenties. New buildings, campus improvements, and anniversaries were all celebrated. When Antilles Field was dedicated on October 19, 1923, the Navy brass was there in all its splendor, headed by Admiral Plunkett. With the Gloria Trumpeters in the lead, students and sailors marched in procession. Up to now, N.J.C. festivals had

James Neilson with honorary degree recipient Corinne Roosevelt Robinson at the 1924 commencement

Cadet battalion participates in the dedication of Antilles Field, October 19, 1923

been consistently blessed with fair weather, but on that day the rains came, and the festivities drew to a bedraggled close with dresses and academic gowns limp and shrunken and mortarboards curled into fantastic shapes. Mr. Loree, who had been largely responsible for all the pomp and circumstance, replaced the ruined mortarboards for the seniors.

At the dedication of the Music Building, five years later, Governor A. Harry Moore of New Jersey gave the principal address. In preparation for the tenth anniversary in May of 1928 invitations were issued to 325 colleges and universities; thirty-nine accepted, ninety-two regretted, and the rest apparently ignored the invitation.[34] At the formal convocation on the anniversary day, May 10, Dean Virginia Gildersleeve of Barnard was the principal speaker. In the afternoon the student body, in appropriate garb, put on a "sokol demonstration," an intricate series of gymnastics of Czecho-

71

The famous Sokol exhibition on the tenth anniversary of the College's founding

Slovak origin, for which they had been drilled by a specialist from that country.[35] The first of its kind in America, the demonstration was recorded in the rotogravure section of the New York *Herald-Tribune* and gave the college wider publicity than anything else in its ten-year history.

The anniversary celebration of 1928 marked a brilliant climax of achievement for the young College and its Dean. Compared to this first decade, the remaining five years of Mrs. Douglass' regime were anticlimactic. For another year the College rode high, reaching a peak enrollment of 1,157 in the autumn of 1929, a figure not equaled until after the Second World War; the state appropriation for that year rose to $430,000. Then the Great Depression struck with its disastrous consequences for all walks of life. Within the next four years enrollment fell off to 961, while the money from the State dropped to $272,000. Funds for new construction had begun to fail earlier, when the confident request for a new physical education building was turned down, and all new building was now out of the question.

At about this time, too, the State began to tighten controls. A legislative commission—the Duffield Commission —had been created in 1928 to inquire into all aspects of the relation of Rutgers University to the State of New Jersey and of N.J.C. to both. Among other things, the commission's report brought forth a new administrative agency, the Board of Regents, with regulatory and fiscal controls over the entire University. Though these new controls interfered considerably with its freedom of action, the College accepted them in good spirit and adjusted to the new dispensation, for in Dean Douglass' words the Duffield report was "fair and just to the university." [36] It was in the original contract with the Board of Regents, by the way, that New Jersey College for Women was officially listed for the first time as one of the "co-ordinate and constituent colleges" of the University, along with the College of Arts and Sciences for men, the College of Agriculture and the College of Engineering. But when the Regents then proceeded to map out a tentative plan for the reorganization of the University in which the status of N.J.C. was left nebulous, anxiety mounted and the College, instead of planning expansion, had to fight to maintain its integrity.

The difficulty was aggravated by increasing disharmony between the administration of the College and that of the University. Dean Douglass had got on very well on the whole with President Demarest, but not with his successor, John M. Thomas. The latter, an ardent advocate of full state university status for Rutgers, was critical of the College for Women, charging it with overemphasis on physical expansion at the cost of academic excellence and administra-

John Martin Thomas, President of Rutgers,
1925–1930

tive efficiency, and accusing it of hiring cheap labor. This though N.J.C. had deliberately tightened academic standards in recent years, had been awarding Phi Beta Kappa honors since 1922, and was approved by the Association of American Universities. The salary scale, to be sure, was lower than that of Rutgers.[37]

In the face of these mounting pressures, the Dean's position was clear. She favored continuance of contractual relations with the state and was willing to accept increasing controls as an inevitable consequence of continuing financial support. At the same time she wished to remain in the Rutgers family, but as an affiliated college with its own faculty, administration, and budget, which "will cooperate wholeheartedly with all other divisions but will be completely autonomous." [38] In this stand she had the full support of the State Federation of Women's Clubs, which made its views unmistakable in a resolution presented to the Trustees:

Whatever the ultimate reorganization of the State University of New Jersey, the State Federation of Women's Clubs urges that instead of being merged into a coeducational institution, the Women's College shall maintain its identity as a college for women, and in its development and management shall be autonomous.[39]

With even greater enthusiasm, the students rallied to the support of their alma mater and the vindication of its integrity. A letter from the Cooperative Government Association to the trustees stated their position as follows:

We the students of New Jersey College for Women, wish to express . . . our appreciation and regard for this institution as it stands at present. Our campus, professors, traditions, and general relationships have come to mean much in our college lives, although the college is young; and we cherish the wholesome spirit of companionship and cooperation which prevails among us. We sincerely hope this simple statement of our respect for the achievements so far attained will convey to you our love and esteem for our alma mater.[40]

In the midst of the deepening Depression, and with the controversies over the relation to Rutgers and the State still unresolved, the regime of Dean Douglass came to a close. The tremendous pressures of the past fifteen years, coupled with family tragedy and personal sorrows, had undermined her health. In the spring of 1930 she remained away from her office for several months because of illness, then returned to conduct the affairs of the College for two more years, until June of 1932. That was the end. She was given a year's leave of absence, but failing to recover her strength she resigned on July 1, 1933.

The retirement of Dean Douglass called forth an outburst of sentiment extraordinary for its volume and the sincerity of its tone. The letters that poured in on her were not conventional platitudes but were filled with expressions of genuine regret and esteem. Dr. Demarest was voicing the sense of the community when in the official resolution of appreciation he regretted her retirement "from what is in so real a sense your own creation and what has so completely depended upon you day by day for fifteen years." James Neilson, who had been such a tower of strength from the beginning but also at times her severest critic, wrote a long warm letter of praise in which he reviewed her entire career. From faculty members, not given to sentimental effusions, came heartfelt tributes: "Deep personal affection . . . your unfailing consideration and generosity." And again: "You *are* N.J.C. and always will be. Not until it becomes Douglass College . . . will your work have been adequately recognized." And finally from the students, to whom she had meant most: "There has been something missing this year —a presence almost undefinable. . . . We wanted you in chapel, at banquets, at social functions, and in your office. . . . Thank God for having had you." [41]

She did not long survive the separation from her College. That summer and fall she withdrew to her cottage on Lake Placid in the Adirondacks for a long rest. There, on a day in October, she set out in her small boat presumably to gather autumn foliage for the house, as visitors were expected. She never returned from that trip. The empty boat was found later, but not its occupant, who was lost in the icy depths of the lake. [42]

~~~ *3*

Frugal Years

The decade of the nineteen-thirties was in many ways the antithesis of the 'twenties. As the Depression deepened in the land and additional thousands joined the ranks of the unemployed month after month, N.J.C., like all American colleges, had to trim sail to weather the economic storm. Instead of growth and expansion, of building programs and new professorships, the concern now was to make ends meet and keep losses to a minimum. Student enrollment, which had been edging toward 1,200, was now with difficulty kept above 900, and did not again pass the 1,000 mark until 1940. Any increase in the cost of tuition or board to meet the ensuing loss of revenue was out of the question at a time of falling prices and wages. By 1937 the Trustees did venture to raise the general college fee from the $150 set in the nineteen-twenties to $195, but the cost of room and board was not changed.

There was some loss of endowment income through the default of a few bonds in the market crash. But a distinct improvement in the financial position came in 1939. At that time all the annoying separate mortgages on the small residences, which fell due at various times and carried interest rates up to 6 per cent, were paid off with a $500,000 loan from the National Life Insurance Company at 3½ per cent with a 3 per cent annual amortization. This refinancing program, together with the income from the remaining endowment, gave some relief from the hand-to-mouth deficit financing of the previous years.[1]

At the same time the College was kept on short rations by the State. The legislature, harassed by falling revenues and increased expenditure for unemployment relief, was in no mood to be lavish in its annual grants to the women's college; even so it did increase the appropriations somewhat after the low mark of 1932, and compared to what was happening in some other states N.J.C. did not fare too badly. The city of New Brunswick, with revenue troubles of its own, was reluctant to furnish a tax-exempt institution with municipal services which, in a more prosperous era, might have been given without question. Thus, when the College asked for a much-needed traffic light at the corner of George Street and Nichol Avenue, permission was given after some delay provided the college would pay the $1,699 required for installation.[2]

Financial stability was not promoted by the continuing controversy over the relation of the University to the State. Though the Board of Regents now had to sanction all Rutgers budget requests, there were still considerable segments of the population who believed that the University should either be taken over completely or else cut off from all subsidies and returned to private status. Among the plans for the solution of the problem there was one which, if enacted, would have cut N.J.C. off entirely from its Rutgers connection. This was the proposal of the Regents, in 1935, that the land-grant units of Rutgers—the College of Agriculture, the College of Engineering, and the College for Women—together with the State Teachers' Colleges, be combined into a state university, while the original Rutgers College would be set adrift to become again the private college it once had been. Nothing came of this.[3]

On campus, the expansive mood of the 'twenties was giving way to one of economy and retrenchment. An editorial in *Campus News* in 1931 commended the sophomore class for giving up its class luncheon at the Hotel Pennsylvania in New York in favor of a simpler and cheaper meal at Cooper Hall; it also suggested a five-dollar sweater suit as more appropriate for concerts and lectures than the formal wear on which Dean Douglass was still insisting.[4] Retrenchment took other forms. In 1934, twenty residences on Douglass and Gibbons campuses were closed, as was one of the large dining rooms in Cooper; two units of Jameson followed later. Forty-two per cent of the dormitory space was now unoccupied. Commuting students had increased to over one-third of the total enrollment. Applications for admission dropped 50 per cent from 1933 to 1934.[5] The faculty was trimmed down to meet these shrinkages, not by the dismissal of experienced professors, but largely by the elimination of instructorships when the terms of incumbents ended. The reduction of dormitory occupants brought an indirect benefit to the faculty in the form of relief from the crowded offices in which most of them had hitherto been forced to work and meet students in conference. Two buildings on Jameson Campus were converted into offices and for some years, until increasing enrollment after the war

Frugal Years

Campus News

squeezed them out again, the faculty of N.J.C. lived officially in a style to which they had not been accustomed.

A comprehensive program of student aid was initiated in
the early 'thirties and continued throughout the emergency.
The Voorhees Fund—the College's one ace-in-the-hole—
was drawn upon for loans and scholarships. Part-time jobs
were created wherever possible. In the autumn of 1932, 163
students who formerly had not needed help applied for such
jobs, and work was found for ninety-nine of them. More
funds became available when the Federal Government established the National Youth Administration as a New Deal
agency to help fight the Depression. Thereafter, most of the
student aid was financed through NYA funds administered
by the College's Personnel Bureau, headed by Fredericka
Belknap. Fluctuating from year to year, these funds ran as
high as $1,800 a month.[6] The work was of many kinds:
some students were assigned to routine chores in the dormitories or clerical help in offices; others were professional
assistants in the academic departments or waitresses in the
dining halls, the latter still ably presided over by Emma S.
Jobbins. Departmental assistantships carried the highest prestige, but waitress jobs were much sought after because of
their regular hours and relatively high wages. Senior waitress
captains often included the best scholars and outstanding
student leaders. Average pay for these NYA jobs was thirty
to forty cents per hour, and no one was allowed to work
more than seventeen hours a week.

Prominent among those helping the College survive the
Depression were the alumnae. Few in number and not af-
fluent, they exerted themselves with vigor. The Associate
Alumnae, founded by the class of '22 and ardently supported
by Dean Douglass, established a journal, the *Alumnae Bul-*

letin, in 1926 and created the office of paid secretary in 1931.[7] Associate Alumnae relations with the College were cordial from the beginning, and the editor of the *Bulletin* and the secretary of the association were *ex officiis* admitted to faculty meetings. The association, which had organized clubs (or groups) in a number of counties, gave dances and bridge and theater benefits for student aid. It also began systematic giving to its alma mater for a variety of purposes.

Alumnae were particularly helpful—especially those teaching in the high schools of New Jersey—in directing bright girls to N.J.C. and establishing contacts with the schools. Such contacts were necessary if the classrooms and dormitories were to be kept filled with students of high quality. A college officer paid regular visits to high schools and, in addition, made arrangements with local alumnae for meetings known as High School Nights. On a given evening, well advertised in advance, alumnae teachers in the high schools of a county or region would bring interested students together with their parents to a central locale, where another group of alumnae was busy setting up the meeting and preparing refreshments. Meantime, a team from the college had driven up from New Brunswick, including a staff member called the Field Secretary, the first of whom was Eunice DeClark Davidson '31, a faculty member, and one or two attractive seniors. They furnished the program. The Field Secretary talked of practical matters, the professor extolled the glories of a liberal education, the senior portrayed the duties and pleasures of campus life, and a moving picture reel presented glimpses of college activities. The evening ended with informal discussion and get-acquainted talk over cider and doughnuts.

The great advantage of meetings of this kind lay in the

personal touch. Whereas on official daytime visits to the high schools the college officer had to appear at a formal meeting and compete with representatives of dozens of other colleges, on these cozy High School Nights N.J.C. had the audience all to itself. And so the College's task forces traversed the state from Sussex to Cape May, all through the Depression decade, in snow and rain and gloom of night. Exactly how many students were gained was never statistically determined; but the troupe always got back safely, even on one miserable night when coming home on highway U.S. 1 in a dense fog the driver found herself going south in a northbound lane. In 1934–35, a typical year, there were twenty-four such high school evenings, and in addition the college Field Secretary made 106 daytime visits to high schools, all but twenty of them in New Jersey.[8]

To encourage girls to remain in college, the Personnel Bureau initiated a series of annual vocational information conferences, beginning in 1937. Typical was a conference in November of 1939. It began with an evening assembly in Voorhees Chapel which was addressed by Mrs. Chase Going Woodhouse, Director of the Institute of Women's Professional Relations. This was followed by two days of round tables on the opportunities for college women in banking, editing and publishing, fashion and dress design, government, home economics, libraries, merchandising, personnel, secretarial, social work, speech and drama, teaching, and finally "marriage and a career." Each round table had a faculty and a student chairman, and students attended as their class schedules permitted. Women who had won success in each of these fields, including as many alumnae as could be found, led the discussions.

When Dean Douglass gave up active direction of the Col-

lege at the close of the academic year in 1932, the Trustees
appointed a member of the faculty, Albert E. Meder, Jr.,
as Acting Dean. He held this post from June of 1932 to the
spring of 1934. Meder, an assistant professor of mathematics,
had come to N.J.C. from Columbia University in 1926.
Dean Douglass soon recognized his keen logical mind and
unusual administrative gifts and came to lean on him more
and more as the burdens of administration grew heavier,
finally making him Assistant to the Dean in 1929. The
faculty was pleased with his selection as Acting Dean, and
some of his colleagues would have been happy to see him

Albert E. Meder, Jr., of the Mathematics Department,
served as Acting Dean from 1932 to 1934, and later became Vice-Provost and Dean of the University

permanently in that office. But as it was generally assumed that the top administrative post should be held by a woman, the Trustees' committee headed by Mr. Loree—the faculty were not consulted—set about choosing a suitable successor to Dean Douglass.

Their choice fell on Margaret Trumbull Corwin, Executive Secretary of the Graduate School of Yale. Miss Corwin was born in Philadelphia of colonial New England stock; she was graduated from Bryn Mawr College, did war work in France in 1918, then was on the staff of the Yale University Press before advancing to the position in the Graduate School. Throughout her professional life she was active in the American Association of University Women and particularly in the international federation associated with it. Temperament and circumstances gave the twenty-one-year administration of Dean Corwin a different flavor from that of her predecessor. The glitter and flamboyance of the Douglass years were now muted into a lower key, for the new Dean of the College was free from ostentation and unassuming to the point of self-effacement. Instead of outward expansion, the Corwin years emphasized internal improvement. She stood for a liberal education in the traditional sense and, when not thwarted by budgetary stringency, worked to raise standards and promote excellence in all departments of the college. Though she was not a polished public speaker, her addresses to students and colleagues were pleasingly phrased, solid with substance, and singularly free of the clichés and platitudes so common among educators. By way of bringing academic regularity into the shrewd but often capricious hiring-and-firing policies of the first Dean, she worked through channels, consulted her department chairmen on

Margaret Trumbull Corwin, Dean of the College,
1934–1955

staff and policy and did not go over their heads with showy appointments and spectacular programs.

Relations with Rutgers improved under the new Dean. Miss Corwin worked closely and, on the whole, harmoniously with Robert C. Clothier, who had become President of the University the year before she came to N.J.C. At this time, too, it was the President of the University and not Mr. Loree who sat as chairman of the Trustees' Committee, and the Dean's annual reports were addressed to him. Near the end of her administration she looked back on her early years in office as a time when the College sought general accreditation and learned to know itself. She encouraged and took pride in the scholarly achievements of the faculty, called their publications to the attention of the trustees and pleaded with the latter for aid to individual members who planned further research and writing.[9]

Aware of the need of support from outside the campus, Dean Corwin kept in close touch with the Associate Alumnae and the State Federation of Women's Clubs. But as her greatest achievement she held the College together and kept it on an even keel through two difficult decades of economic depression, world war, and post-war adjustment. "A campus devoted to plain living and high thinking"[10] was her first impression of N.J.C., and she proposed to keep it that way. In the opinion of the College Bursar, who worked closely with her in these matters, no one could know with what patience and skill the Dean managed to squeeze educational performance of high quality out of the meager funds available to her from year to year.[11] "Making do" became a fine art under Dean Corwin. Adversity had no terrors for her. Shrinking enrollments and budget cuts merely challenged her ingenuity. "Welcome to another frugal year," was her

Robert Clarkson Clothier, President of Rutgers,
1932–1951

cheerful greeting to the returning faculty at the opening of a new academic year. No other words could better describe the character of the Corwin era.

The faculty who worked with the new Dean was young, as professorial age went. One by one the elder statesmen of Rutgers had withdrawn after a decade or more of faithful and sometimes distinguished service. By 1933 only one department still retained a Rutgers chairman. This was mathematics, where the beloved Richard S. ("Dickie") Morris, who had been there from the beginning, continued to teach until 1944, when he finally retired. A few, like Eugene E. Agger, chairman of the Economics Department, kept up social contacts; he and his wife retained membership in Red Pine, the faculty social club, for another thirty years. But with these few exceptions the faculty had become a separate body, autonomous and distinct from Rutgers. The students in these years used to complain, not altogether facetiously, that the faculty was too normal. They felt cheated at not having at least a few graybearded "characters" to joke about with affectionate pride. Characters or not, some of the hundreds who were members of the faculty at one time or another must be mentioned in these pages. No history of the college would be complete without them.[12]

Some of Dean Douglass' administrative staff held faculty rank and played an important part in College affairs. Alice Aronoff came in 1918 as instructor in physical education. Three years later she was made Assistant to the Dean and continued in this office until her retirement in 1953. "Assistant to the dean" did not begin to describe her manifold activities. She served as recording secretary to the Trustees' Committee, and had the thankless task of compiling the annual catalogue. She supervised the Yule Log Ceremony and song contests generally, where she was a stickler for form and punctilio. Fanatically loyal to the college and its traditions, some of which she had helped create, she was not given to wide and easy friendships. From the vantage point of her cubbyhole office in the tower of College Hall she could survey the comings and goings of administration, faculty, and students. In all seasons the window next to her desk remained open, a device suitable no doubt for a former physical education instructor but also convenient for terminating tedious interviews.

Two other long-time occupants of College Hall offices and pillars of the administration were the Bursar and the Registrar. After Alfred Henderson had resigned as Bursar, he was succeeded by his assistant, Chester W. Snedeker. For two decades Mr. Snedeker filled this sensitive post with ability and tact. Working closely with Dean Corwin, he fought the annual battle of the budget and took on the recurring and unpopular burden of explaining cuts and shortages to frustrated professors. In charge of the physical plant, he maintained an alert and competent staff headed by friendly Earle G. Van Derveer, and a chef's crew directed by Joseph E. Lasagna, which served palatable food in Cooper year after year. Good-natured and approachable, Mr. Snedeker remained popular with students and faculty—quite an achievement for a college financial officer. His untimely death in 1963 left a big hole.

Quietly efficient Esther W. Hawes became Registrar after Mrs. Greene left. Understaffed and without the aid of computers, the Registrar's office prepared increasingly complicated class schedules, compiled grades, and did the thousand-and-one chores that fell to its lot. Unruffled and with constant good humor, Miss Hawes would chide careless students who had misread instructions, ride herd on dilatory professors who were late with their grades, and come to the end of the year with everything in apple-pie order. She retired in 1952.

Mrs. Douglass had early decided that the small but rapidly growing book collection needed a professional librarian in charge. Accordingly, in 1923 she brought in Ada J. English, who was College Librarian to her retirement in 1954. A vigorous administrator, outspoken in her views, Mrs. English with her staff succeeded unusually well in meeting the wishes of a faculty who seldom reached consensus as to the best way of managing a college library.

Among the many staff pioneers, too, was Mary Maud Thompson, R.N., director of the Infirmary for thirty-one years. She came in 1920 and saw the Infirmary grow from one room in Cooper Hall in which she lived and provided a cot for a possible patient to a three-story building, excellently equipped and staffed. When she retired in 1951 she said she had "none but the most pleasant memories of association with students and faculty," and they felt the same about her and her capabilities.

The first full-time professor in arts and sciences not from Rutgers but appointed directly to the N.J.C. faculty was Ira D. Garard. Freshly discharged from overseas service in chemical warfare, Garard came in 1919 to teach chemistry and to supervise the development of the science program. A disciplinarian who considered higher education a serious business, he ran a taut department. In chemistry courses there was no fooling around; students had to work hard to pass and high grades were a rarity. Yet when he discovered an intelligent student really trying, he was ready with time and patience to help her find her way. Garard was one of the closest confidants of Dean Douglass, who relied heavily on his judgment. Not the least of his services was that of devil's advocate in faculty meetings, where he fearlessly espoused unpopular causes and punctured easy sentimental assumptions which his colleagues had not always bothered to subject to critical analysis. Throughout his career—he retired in 1957—he remained a dominant figure in the intellectual life of the campus. He was succeeded in the chairmanship by Roger S. Sweet, who had come in 1931, left for a post in industry during the Second World War, and returned to academic life six years later. Sweet too kept standards high and battled for values and goals similar to his predecessor's.

In the biological sciences Jessie G. Fiske was the earliest. Beginning as a laboratory assistant in botany in 1918, she advanced through the ranks to ultimate full professorship and chairmanship of her department. An accomplished equestrienne, Miss Fiske owned a string of horses which enriched the physical activities program when riding was still one of the sports a student could select and Crop and Spur, with its riding track where Hickman Hall rose later, was an active campus organization. She contributed to the lighter side of campus life with her torch songs in the faculty shows of the 'forties and 'fifties. She retired in 1960.

First chairman of the Zoology Department was Leon A. Hausman, an ornithologist of note, with many publications, scholarly and popular, to his credit. Hausman had another and rather unusual specialty. He was an expert on human hair and was frequently called in as consultant in criminal cases, to confirm clues or to identify victims or suspects. Long a familiar figure on campus, with his cheerful mien, his clipped New England speech, and his black butterfly tie, he retired in 1955. Another New Englander, John A. Small, taught in the Botany Department from 1928 to 1966. His interests also ranged beyond the campus to such things as the preservation of the flora and fauna of New Jersey and the improvement of the schools of his township.

The English Department was the largest in the college. Oral S. Coad, who headed it, came from Columbia University in 1923, was made chairman after Professor Whitman returned to Rutgers and held that office until his retirement in 1958. A specialist in American drama, he had written a biography of William Dunlap and, with a co-author, a volume on the history of the American stage. His courses were always well filled. In the 'twenties Coad assembled a group of younger colleagues who remained together, with some changes and additions, into the 'fifties. Raymond Bennett, Donald and Edith Dorian, Eva Loudon, and Fred Rockwell made up this core. Though not in agreement on all subjects—Miss Loudon was by no means a docile disciple of her chairman—their longevity alone gave to English a continuity and a character shared by no other department. Along with Ira Garard, Oral Coad was one of the two elder statesmen who was entrusted with important missions and whose opinions carried great weight. He defied labeling as either a categorical conservative or liberal, for though he valued tradition he was independent in his judgments. On more than one occasion he championed individuals and minorities against the weight of authority. In retirement he has busied himself with writing in the literary history of New Jersey.

Donald C. Dorian, a Milton scholar, was one of the most valuable members of the faculty, serving as chairman of the important Committee on Admissions, then for six years as

Dean of Instruction, finally as chairman of the English Department. Thoroughness and integrity characterized everything he undertook, and his relations with his colleagues were marked by an old-fashioned courtesy. One of the seven teaching faculty members to receive a Rutgers University Medal for Distinguished Service, he retired in 1962 and died less than a year later.

When, in the mid-twenties, women's organizations throughout New Jersey began to complain that not enough

Faculty members with twenty-five or more years of service, photographed in 1952. Seated: Dr. Jessie G. Fiske, Botany; Helena M. Kees, Physical Education; Dr. Leon A. Hausman, Zoology; Dr. Zora Klain, Education. Standing: Dr. Ira D. Garard, Chemistry; Wilda M. Long, Physical Education; Raymond E. Rudy, Music; Evelyn J. Hawkes, Education; Dr. Donald C. Dorian, English; Dr. Oral S. Coad, English

women of high professional caliber were being given an op-
portunity on the faculty of the state's college for women,
Dean Douglass went out into the marketplace to bring in
such people. Prominent among them were Shirley Smith,
Jane Inge, Alice W. De Visme, Helen W. Hazen, and Emily
G. Hickman. Miss Smith, an Oberlin graduate with a Ph.D.
from Yale, entered the then flourishing Classics Department.
Upon the withdrawal of the Rutgers professors of Latin and
Greek she became chairman, a position she held until her retirement in 1960. It was not a rewarding post, for Greek and
Latin at N.J.C., as in American colleges generally, were fight-
ing a losing battle, and Miss Smith's tenure of office was one
long continuous rearguard action. Other teaching positions in
the classics were abandoned as enrollment fell away, and in
her last years she remained the only representative in the entire College of those fields of learning which had once been
the mainstay of all higher education. Cheerful and un-
daunted, she continued to proclaim the ancient wisdom on
which the whole liberal culture of the West was reared,
meeting her classes and showing her lantern slides in her
large breezy office and classroom—the one-time kitchen of
the old Carpender House—and fought the good fight to the
end. Ironically, the tide in the classics began to turn at about
this point, and under her successors Greek and Latin enrollments began again to grow.

Jane Inge was the dramatic chairman of the Department
of Speech and Dramatic Art, originally a subdivision of the
English Department. In the Little Theater, where she
reigned supreme, she presented three plays a year for the
general public, with the aid of a loyal and capable staff.
Talented and temperamental, she undertook unbelievable
quantities of work and expected her students to do the same.

Until curbed by the Dean of Students, Mrs. Inge's play re-hearsals lasted far into the night. Immensely versatile, she directed the plays, planned the sets, designed and helped sew costumes. She was a stickler for technique and drill and had only contempt for sentimentalists who urged her to let the girls express themselves. Even if they had any-thing to express, so she believed, they were incapable of communicating their thoughts and emotions on the stage without thorough discipline in the fundamentals of voice production, enunciation, and body control. Mrs. Inge was a highly successful teacher, for she knew exactly what re-sults she was after and she got those results. After retirement she moved to Plainfield, New Jersey, where she continued to direct plays.

Alice W. De Visme came from Middlebury College to teach French. Born and educated in France, she was instru-mental in establishing the French language house, the *Ile de France*, and was for many years chairman of her de-partment. Throughout her long career, Madame De Visme upheld the best traditions of French culture. In this she was ably seconded by Marguerite Lentz Richards, also French-born and educated, but with an American Ph.D. in addition. Beginning as an instructor in 1928, Mrs. Richards rose in time to a full professorship and served a term as department chairman. Interested in educational issues beyond the con-fines of one department, she participated effectively in gen-eral college affairs. She served an even wider constituency when, during the Second World War, she was sent to France by the United States Office of Strategic Services.

Manuel Salas was for many years the key man in Spanish. A member of the faculty from 1929 to 1965, he was chair-man of the Department of Romance Languages for fifteen of those years. He published a number of pedagogic and literary works; his wife, a former student of his, collaborated in some of these. Then there was William Oncken. Born and educated in Switzerland, Oncken was like so many of his countrymen fluent in three languages, but he taught mainly Italian. In Princeton, where he lived for years, he was occasionally mistaken for Albert Einstein, whom Oncken resembled in appearance.

Another language professor who married an alumna was Emil Jordan of the German Department. An economist by training, with degrees from the Universities of Königsberg and Berlin, Jordan taught at N.J.C. from 1931 to 1966, for the last two-thirds of this span as department chairman. Though also an author of textbooks in his field, he was more widely known for his *Nature Atlas of America*. Associated with him in the department for many years was Alice Schlimbach, affectionately remembered by many German majors as director of *Das Deutsche Haus*.

One of the most dynamic individuals on the N.J.C. faculty was Emily G. Hickman, a historian with a Ph.D. from Cornell. Arriving in 1928 and immediately given full professorial rank, Miss Hickman rose rapidly to the upper echelons and was entrusted with highly responsible administrative duties by Dean Douglass. This did not prove a congenial arrangement, for the Dean and the new history professor failed to see eye to eye on many matters, and the latter's advance up the administrative ladder was brought to a sudden stop. Thwarted in this ambition and too full of ideas and energy to be satisfied with routine teaching, Miss Hickman threw herself into civic activities. She was asked to join the national board of the Y.W.C.A.; she interested herself in international affairs and eventually became chairman for the State of New Jersey of the National Committee on the Cause and Cure of War. Determined and outspoken, Miss Hickman, whose younger years had witnessed the culmination of the woman suffrage crusade, never entirely lost the militancy of the embattled feminist. In great demand as a public lecturer she spent much time away from campus, a practice common enough in large universities, but almost unknown in N.J.C. at that time. With all her outside activities she did not neglect her academic duties. Her classes were stimulating and her courses were elected by students ready for intellectual adventure. History was for her a means to an end: understanding the present and controlling the future. With this in mind, she organized her courses in unorthodox ways. When asked by a colleague how she managed to get her section of freshmen through the medieval portion of the crowded introductory course ahead of all the other instructors, she replied: "I left out the Church." An editorial in the college newspaper at the time of her death in 1947 summed up student opinion: you don't know what higher education is unless you have had a course with Miss Hickman. The new classroom and office building, Hickman Hall, was fittingly named in her honor.

The history faculty was expanded in 1928 by the arrival of Anna M. Campbell and Margaret A. Judson. The former, a medievalist, was elected to the British Royal Society for her book: *The Black Death and Men of Learning;* the latter specialized in seventeenth-century England and her *Crisis of the Constitution* was a notable contribution in this field. Miss Judson was to become one of the most influential members of the faculty. In 1966, when about to retire, she was asked to serve as Acting Dean following the resignation of Dean Ruth M. Adams, and filled this post with vigor and distinction. In 1930 George P. Schmidt joined the department and remained for thirty years. For twenty of those he was chairman of the Department of History and Political Science. He taught American history with emphasis on social and cultural factors; his field of research and publication was the history of American higher education.

When Eugene E. Agger of Rutgers relinquished his courses at the College along with the chairmanship of the Department of Economics and Sociology, he was replaced by Francis W. Hopkins, who continued on the faculty until his retirement in 1962, and served from 1932 to 1958 as chairman of this large and vital department. Besides teaching large numbers of students and keeping his department on an even keel, Hopkins, a specialist in taxation, took an active interest in economic and political issues in community and state. Noted for sanity and sound judgment, his was a respected voice in faculty and administration. Because economists and sociologists were in demand in other fields, it was difficult to secure and keep good people in this department, and until salaries were stabilized and improved after the Second World War, its turnover was considerable. The only long-term colleague of Hopkins was Miriam E. West, a specialist in labor problems.

Chairman of the Psychology Department was Sidney A. Cook, a war veteran like Garard; Cook also headed the entire social science division during the years when that administrative arrangement was in force. Philosophy, originally bracketed with psychology and never a large department, had one mainstay, William J. Norton, from 1930 to 1963. In his teaching Norton did not make a fetish of analysis and methodology, but remained always the humanist. Though philosophy majors were few, his courses appealed, year after year, to many of the better students from other departments.

Continuity and little turnover characterized the Mathematics Department, at least until after the Second World War. After Richard Morris of Rutgers retired in 1944, Cyril A. Nelson, who had been on the staff since 1927, succeeded as Chairman and held the post until his own retirement in 1959. In addition to his teaching—he also offered a course in astronomy for a time—Nelson was chairman of the Library Committee and was involved for many years, along with Mrs. English and others, in the seemingly hopeless task of drawing plans for a library building of the future, plans that did not come to fruition until after his retirement. Robert M. Walter, a Rutgers graduate, came in 1929 as instructor and eventually became department chairman succeeding Nelson. Musically gifted, Walter was in demand for arrangements of musical scores for Junior Show and, later, for the quadrennial faculty shows.

The professional departments contributed talent and variety to the faculty roster. Taking over the Department of Health and Physical Education in the mid-twenties, Helena M. Kees guided its fortunes for over thirty years. Thirty years in the packing-box Gymnasium with all its frustrations and inadequacies failed to quench the fresh enthusiasm which Miss Kees brought to her office. Interested in her students and in the problems of higher education far beyond her special field, she was a valued and respected member of the faculty. Despite limited facilities, she introduced innovations into the physical education program and she carried her interest in health and recreation into the service of the larger New Brunswick community.

Helen W. Hazen headed the Home Economics Department, which had figured so prominently in the founding of the

College, from 1927 to 1953. For a quarter-century she directed the varied program in foods and nutrition, textiles, fashions, home furnishings, and family relations which the department gradually built up. Another member of this department, gratefully remembered by hungry professors and commuting students, was Mary I. Raven, whose laboratory cafeteria served a noon meal to the college community. The food here was of the highest quality and tastefully prepared. For the faculty the place provided relaxation, a chance to hear campus gossip, and to exchange views on college problems and policies. More than one measure, formally adopted later in faculty meeting, was hatched in the home economics cafeteria. It succumbed in 1966, several years after Miss Raven had retired.

From the earliest years, music and the Music Department played a prominent role in the life of N.J.C. This was especially true after the erection of the Music Building and of Voorhees Chapel. Competent artists manned its faculty; its chairman was Canadian-born J. Earle Newton. As chapel organist and choir director, Newton enriched the cultural experience of students and faculty; as head of a varied and difficult department he laid the foundations of excellence on which later chairmen could build. With remarkable ingenuity he arranged liturgical music for the use of the choir and brought out purity and brilliance in its voices. Above all, he managed to engender in his students a love and understanding of music and thus contributed to their liberal education in the highest sense of the word. To hear the chapel choir, whether at regular assemblies, at Sunday vespers, or at their special concerts, was always a moving experience.

Among Newton's colleagues, the one with the longest

An art class of the 'thirties in the attic of Recitation—
now Arts—Building

term of service was Raymond E. Rudy. He too came in the
first decade and stayed into the fifth. He taught organ and
also conducted the Glee Club. In addition to his college
duties Rudy was organist at Trinity Church in Princeton.
An early alumna to find a permanent position on the N.J.C.
faculty was a member of the Music Department: Stephanie
Morris Marryott '25. She taught piano and music appreciation, and also helped keep the tradition of "the singing college" alive by coaching a popular singing group, the Weepies, and helping with the musical scores of the annual Junior
Show.

Ethel M. Fair, a professional librarian of stature, directed
the Library School from 1930 to 1950. In the face of considerable difficulties, mostly financial, she and her staff turned
out an annual quota of well-trained librarians during those
two decades. After leaving N.J.C., Professor Fair took on a

Fulbright assignment in Cairo, Egypt, and then continued her professional activities in various institutions.

Since a large percentage of every graduating class was trained to teach in the schools of New Jersey, the Department of Education took on great importance. Its members were Zora Klain, chairman, Evelyn J. Hawkes, and Dorothy Waldo. When, in 1956, the department was merged with the University Graduate School of Education, one member was designated as coordinator on the women's college campus.

Mavericks and birds of passage were rare at N.J.C. Julian Moreno-Lacalle, debonair favorite of Mrs. Douglass, scintillated briefly in Romance Languages. John A. Rice, Rhodes scholar and stormy petrel of the American academic world, taught for two years in the Classics Department before going on to Rollins and eventually to his own experimental Black Mountain College. Dean Corwin's activities in the International Federation of University Women brought an occasional European scholar to the campus. Dr. Erna Patzelt, a medievalist from the University of Vienna, joined the History Department as visiting professor for the second semester in 1938. She added prestige, was a stimulating lecturer and well liked by her colleagues and her students. Dr. Ida Bobula, Hungarian scholar and war refugee, came for a semester in 1948 and taught an unusual course: a history of the social and economic position of women in Western culture, beginning with ancient Greece. Faculty as well as students attended her lectures.[13]

Under the leadership of the men and women sketched in the preceding pages, the faculty became an efficient instrument providing a well-thought-out program of higher education for a carefully selected student body. Homogeneous and committed to the welfare of the College as a whole, the faculty offered little opportunity to departmental empire builders. Jealous of its prerogatives, it conscientiously nurtured all the powers vested in it by the trustees. To avoid hasty action, it refused to vote finally on any measure not included in the formal agenda distributed well in advance of every meeting. In the nineteen-sixties the waiting period between first introduction of a policy measure and final vote was further enlarged.

As in American colleges generally, the faculty conducted its business by means of a comprehensive committee system. The powerful Curriculum Committee screened all proposed changes in general program and departmental course offerings; its recommendations were seldom overruled. The Academic Regulations Committee reviewed the never-ending procession of cases of individual students. Until the weight of numbers, by the late nineteen-fifties, made such detailed supervision impossible, the faculty insisted on discussing and resolving each case and rejected all motions to delegate final decisions to the committee or to administrative agencies.

The Committee on Admission and the Underclass Years, under the chairmanship of Albert Meder, who returned to faculty ranks after the accession of Dean Corwin, performed the difficult feat of keeping up the numbers of entering students without lowering standards. Throughout these difficult years, when college enrollments suffered everywhere, the freshman classes were consistently selected from the top quarter of New Jersey high school senior classes, with a sizable fraction in the top 10 per cent and a fair sprinkling of valedictorians and salutatorians. After Meder left the College to move into the higher echelons of University administration in 1943, Donald Dorian of the English

Department conducted the committee with the same high standards and the same meticulous attention to each applicant. Criteria for admission were multiple: the applicant's high school grades and extra-curricular record, recommendations from her principal, teachers and others who knew her, a personal interview and, after 1935, her score in the Scholastic Aptitude Test set by the College Entrance Examination Board. In a general reorganization of the committee system in 1936 a Committee on Educational Policies was added, to keep abreast of developments in higher education and call the faculty's attention to desirable innovations.[14]

For five years, beginning in 1929, the academic departments were grouped under four division chairmen, one each for the sciences, the humanities, the social sciences, and the professional departments. The arrangement was not a success. It was a mechanical device, and there were complaints over the unnatural alliance of departments that had little in common. Besides, it was expensive. And so, to the general satisfaction, the division system was quietly buried in 1934, ostensibly as an economy measure.

Concern for the individual student did not end with the Committee on Admission but was characteristic of the faculty as a whole. Since participation in the University's graduate program had been discouraged, the professor who poured all his research and scholarship into his graduate seminar to the neglect of his other students was practically nonexistent. The importance of conferences with his students was impressed on every new instructor, and an uncommonly large segment of each department chairman's time was given to the counseling of his majors. Faculty members were constantly speaking to, or arranging programs for, the many student clubs: *Campus News* was full of such notices, week after week. The students liked this and expressed a desire for wider social contacts with the faculty as well. These social affairs, while pleasant enough, were not always allowed to develop naturally but tended to become over-formalized. At one time a special committee was set up to arrange regularly scheduled teas in the commuters' center, the Beehive, at which professors could meet students, the faculty to rotate attendance in groups of ten.[15] And this was not the only such occasion.

While the undergraduates were its first concern, the faculty was not allowed to lose sight of its obligation to the State of New Jersey and especially to the women of the State. The College owed much to the State Federation of Women's Clubs, and local clubs from Sussex to Cape May were encouraged both by Dean Douglass and Dean Corwin to draw on faculty talent for their programs. The Music Department was soon in great demand for recitals, and the Art Department for illustrated lectures. The social scientists discussed the international scene or contemporary problems of American life, members of the English Department reviewed books and authors, and the scientists undertook the difficult task of interpreting important advances in their fields to laymen. Not only women's clubs, but Parent-Teacher Associations, church groups, Rotary, Kiwanis, and Lions made use of the N.J.C. faculty speakers' roster.

Unheralded and largely unremunerative, this public lecture program, though irregular and haphazard, constituted a statewide service of adult education. In the early nineteen-thirties there was an informal understanding that one might ask a ten-dollar fee without necessarily expecting to get it. On rare occasions a windfall of twenty-five dollars might come one's way; but far more often it was a free service, with possible reimbursement for traveling expenses if a long drive was involved. One long-suffering faculty wife, after seeing her husband go out on the lecture circuit year after year, exclaimed in exasperation that she would one day write an article on free speech at N.J.C. Alumnae Clubs, who liked to have their favorite professors on their programs, always paid expenses and were not expected to contribute anything more.

There were compensations. The lecture program undoubtedly engendered good will toward the College and respect for its intellectual standards. A responsive audience of clubwomen, or high school teachers, or a League of Women Voters group always made the effort seem worth while. It was salutary for college professors, habitually confronted by captive audiences of young people as a sounding board for their ideas, to match their wits with adults whose training and experience were equal to, though different from, their own.

Ludicrous episodes were not wanting. A member of one of the science departments was invited by a club in a neighboring county as a last-minute replacement for a harp soloist from New York who had fallen ill. In presenting the professor, the program chairman used the same introduction she had already written for the musician, even including a joke about a cantankerous harpist who died, went to heaven, and instead of hitting harps with the angels began to hit the angels with his harp, then calmly went on, "But our harpist could not come, and in his stead we have Professor X from N.J.C. who will speak to us on the chemistry of cosmetics." At another time the College lecturer, after sitting through a long business session, then enduring the high school band—in a basement room with a low ceiling—finally had his turn. All through his talk he was aware, along with everybody else, of noisy scraping and whispering and giggling behind a screen off to one side. When he finished, to the usual round of perfunctory applause, the chairman rose: "Thank you, professor. And now we come to the event you have all been waiting for. Little Shirley will do her tap dance for us." And from behind the screen, where she had been held in leash all through the lecture, stepped six-year-old Shirley, in appropriate costume, to bring the meeting to its climax.

In Dean Corwin's day, faculty social functions achieved a pleasant balance between the formal and the informal, differing alike from the stiff protocol of Dean Douglass' regime and the much greater informality of later years. The faculty had its own social club. When the new Music Building was completed, the old frame residence which had housed the Music Department was made available for faculty social use and a club was built around it: the Red Pine Club, pine trees being common on campus. Most of the clubhouse furnishings were donated by Mrs. Eagleton of the Trustees' Committee; other pieces, including a pool table, came from various sources. A formal reception marked the opening on February 15, 1929. The old Red Pine Club furnished many an evening's sociability and entertainment to members and guests, even though the rotating committees in charge of each supper, who prepared the food at home and cleaned up afterward, found the evening more work than pleasure. After the College acquired Wood Lawn, the club was given a room there, along with the privileges of the mansion on social evenings, and the work of the committees became less burdensome, for the Wood Lawn staff now prepared the food and washed the dishes. At Wood Lawn, too, it was possible for individual members to entertain their friends or groups of students, a convenience for unmarried professors living in small apartments. Thus, over the years, the Red Pine Club continued as a morale builder and a unifying influence.

Morale was not lifted by the financial buffetings of the 'thirties. In 1933 the Depression finally caught up with the faculty. In the summer of that year the Trustees reluctantly voted a 10 per cent reduction in salaries. This was bound to come, economic conditions being what they were, yet there was little comfort in the accompanying assurance that the salaries were not subject to the federal income tax. Even so, N.J.C. was not as badly off as many other colleges. No established members of the faculty were dismissed, only instructorships were vacated at the end of the incumbents' one-year term. Then, too, the cost of living was lower. As Irving Berlin had it in the popular song, "potatoes are cheaper, tomatoes are cheaper." So were rents, and clothes, and concert and theater tickets. Good balcony seats could be had to top Broadway plays and musicals for less than two dollars when purchased at cut-rate offices in Times Square.

The course of study that the faculty fashioned and administered reflected prevailing trends in American higher education. It was not far out, either to the right or to the left. The College for Women was "not the first by whom the new was tried nor yet the last to lay the old aside." The guiding principle was that of distribution and concentration: a sampling of many subjects and intensive study of one. Evolving from the simpler program which Dean Douglass and the Rutgers professors who constituted her original faculty had begun in 1918, the curriculum by the mid-nineteen-thirties had the following features:

Frugal Years

Every candidate for the A.B. degree, regardless of her principal interest or field of concentration, was required to take certain broad introductory courses in the freshman and sophomore years. These included English composition, the history of Western civilization, a course each in a physical and a biological science or else one science and a year of mathematics. She also had to take enough work in a foreign language to reach a specified level of proficiency, which meant two years for most students in addition to their courses in high school. A year's course in literature or music or the fine arts, and a year's course in a social science completed the general requirements. By the end of her sophomore year, if not sooner, every student had to select a subject of major interest on which she would concentrate during her last two years. At this midpoint she passed from the academic jurisdiction of the Faculty Committee on the Underclass Years to that of the chairman of her major department, who helped her round out her program with subjects related to her major, plus any others that interested her and for which she could qualify.

This program, which remained unchanged in its aims and essential arrangements for four decades, was supposed to give the graduate a liberal education. This meant, in the broadest terms, that she had made the acquaintance of the leading masterpieces of literature and the arts and through them acquired a cultivated taste and a critical faculty; that she had been introduced to the political, economic, and social institutions of her contemporary world and gained some understanding of the meaning of continuity and change in human affairs; that she knew something of the assumptions and techniques of science and its role in modern life; and finally, that in her major subject she had achieved at least the beginning of expertise and professional competence. This was the doctrine of a liberal education as it was preached and practiced in American colleges with varying degrees of success. How close the graduates of N.J.C. came to realizing the ideal no one will ever know—no one but themselves.

Not every student chose a liberal arts major. A considerable number every year preferred the vocational and preprofessional programs. A girl whose main interest was home economics or journalism found that she could not get quite as rich a fare in the liberal arts because of the demands of a program designed to fit her for gainful employment in her chosen field. This dilution occurred mostly in the upper years; the freshman and sophomore programs were almost the same for vocational as for liberal arts students. In attempting to fit vocational training into an academically oriented curriculum, N.J.C. encountered difficulties common to all liberal arts colleges. The ideal of a liberal education, for all the exalted rhetoric of its devotees, was difficult to maintain in practice in a society where specialized training was almost indispensable for securing employment and earning a living on any but the lowest economic levels. As a result, college administrators, while continuing to pay lip service to the liberal ideal, were increasingly under pressure to give in to vocational demands, and liberal arts majors formed a smaller percentage of the total number of graduates year after year. Women's colleges were better able to resist the trend, for fairly obvious reasons. Women were not as a rule subject to the same long-term vocational pressures as men, traditionally the family breadwinners, and could therefore more freely indulge their taste for literature and the arts, though their future husbands' interest might be just as genuine.

Actually, the choice of a liberal major by students at N.J.C. was not always as disinterested as their professors liked to believe. Sooner or later, the sophomore consulting her prospective department chairman would come up with the question: what can I *do* with English, with history, after I graduate? Or if she did not ask it, her parents did. Four years of college were costly and often represented a real financial sacrifice. To be told that their daughter would graduate with an enlightened grasp of world problems and an elevated taste in literature but would have to scrounge for a job, that seemed to even the most understanding parents a bit quixotic. There was, however, one thing a girl could do with her liberal major: she could teach it. Let her surround the subject of her choice with the requisite number of courses in Education, work in the necessary supervised practice teaching, and she would be eligible for a certificate entitling her to teach in any high school in New Jersey. The four years of liberal education, instead of ending in a blue vapor, could thus lead to a respectable career. In this fashion many a student was saved for the liberal arts.

Whether this was the best way to recruit superior teachers was another question. Love for a subject and thorough understanding of it, while of course indispensable, were not enough. There were other qualities which could make or break a teacher. Elusive and intangible, these were not always easy to detect in a girl of nineteen, yet the faculty felt obligated to make the attempt. In 1939 it set up a screening board, the Committee on Teacher Education, whose purpose it was to weed out obvious incompetents, discourage those who seemed unlikely to succeed as teachers and redirect them into some other course of study. Professors of the arts and sciences were in the majority on this committee, for the faculty believed that the professional education of the future teachers in the student body was the concern of all their instructors, not only of the Department of Education. Students at N.J.C. did not major in Education, as they did in many other colleges, but in the subjects they expected to teach. The Committee was the device for securing cooperation between the subject matter and the professional department. While occasionally mistaken in its prognosis, the Committee operated on the whole with such success that the entire University eventually adopted the system of the College for Women.

Though the general course of study was, as indicated, a fairly standard version of the distribution-concentration pattern, it did present a few distinguishing features. The sciences and mathematics drew a larger percentage of the students than was customary in women's colleges; the Mathematics Department was one of the larger ones and attracted some of the best students. Music and art, subjects commonly emphasized in women's colleges, got off to an uneven start. The former enjoyed one of the finest and best-equipped buildings in the country, while the latter had to make do with one crowded office, one lecture room, and an unfinished attic, all in Recitation (now Arts) Building, which also housed the College Library and classrooms of other departments. Chairman of the Art Department from 1930 to 1953 was Herbert R. Kniffin. Both music and art had to divide their efforts between the practical and the theoretical. The Music Department offered formal instruction in voice, piano, organ, and various orchestral instruments, while the Art Department gave studio work in drawing,

The Music Building, opened in 1928, was the gift of more than one hundred Women's Clubs of the New Jersey State Federation

painting, and graphic arts and design; at the same time both conducted period courses in the history of their subjects and widely popular "appreciation" courses for the student body in general.

From the late nineteen-twenties on, modern languages were taught by what was then an advanced technique. The first objective was a practical speaking knowledge of the language, an indispensable groundwork for later courses in literature. To this end, the use of English was held to a minimum, even in the introductory courses. When one entered a French or a German or a Spanish classroom one heard—and spoke—only that language. To facilitate student

progress and make the exposure to the foreign culture genuine, the departments were staffed exclusively by instructors
born and educated in the country whose language they
taught. Finally, there were the three language houses, *Ile de
France, Das Deutsche Haus,* and *Luzmela,* where the majority of the language majors lived during their junior and
senior years. They also ate at common-language tables in
Cooper, and were expected to speak only the language of
their major at meals.

The advantages of this method were obvious. Foreign languages and cultures came to life; the language houses were
highly successful. There were drawbacks, too. Foreign language instructors, coming and going at a high rate of turnover, did not always grasp American educational needs and
practices as fully as desired. Lacking this familiarity, they

A group of students in Luzmela (Spanish House) in the
'thirties

failed to play the part in faculty affairs or to make the contribution to academic life to which their background and training entitled them. Some, to be sure, managed to adapt European standards to American conditions and became valuable and important members of the college community.

One of the more interesting examples of experimental teaching came from political science, where Harold A. Van Dorn and Mildred Moulton conducted courses in American government, international relations, and welfare problems, not by the time-honored method of formal lecture and recitation, but by group reports based on wide reading in periodical literature as well as contacts with actual political situations in city and state. Such practices were not as common then as now. A radio and record player in the political science classroom was the first in the College used as an educational aid. It was over this radio that students in American history and government first heard the ringing voice of Franklin D. Roosevelt reassuring the American people in his famous first inaugural address that the only thing they had to fear was fear itself.

A dispute over the American Government course led to one of the few instances of open opposition to Dean Douglass both in the faculty and the student body. Until 1931 this course was required of all sophomores, but in that year the Curriculum Committee recommended an enlargement of this requirement to include economics, sociology, and American history as alternatives. Dean Douglass fully approved the change though she had not initiated it. The political science professors resisted it. They had the support of a vocal and militant campus League of Women Voters, which appealed to the Trustees over the heads of the faculty and the Dean, and of *Campus News*, which opened its columns to indignant letters from subscribers and also endorsed the political scientists' position with eloquent editorials. In a straw vote conducted by the paper, all classes except the freshmen overwhelmingly favored the retention of the political science requirement. There were fireworks in the faculty meeting that decided the issue, even though the minutes merely recorded that "after discussion lasting more than an hour" the committee's recommendation was adopted and the political science monopoly came to an end. In the course of this discussion Dean Douglass, nettled at the opposition from student groups and faculty members, had denounced the political scientists as disloyal and insubordinate and demanded that the faculty disavow their position. It did; not out of subservience to the Dean, for there was wide sympathy with their pilloried colleagues, but because it believed the curricular change a sound one.[16]

A prime illustration of faculty concern for the students was furnished by the freshman history course, labeled in the catalogue as Introduction to Contemporary Civilization. Required of all freshmen, the course endeavored to pull out of the past those events, institutions, and trends that seemed most relevant to an understanding of the world of today. It was not unique. Rutgers had a similar course, as did many other colleges; all were adaptations of the omnibus course in contemporary civilization which Columbia University had developed at the end of the First World War. The History Department took its responsibility seriously. The freshmen were not fobbed off on the youngest instructor, but every member of the department, including the chairman, taught at least one of its many sections. Since there was considerable room for differences of opinion as to which events in six thousand years of recorded history were most important for explaining the present, the course suffered many alterations over the years. At one time it began with 1500 A.D. and concentrated on Western Europe; then it went to the other extreme and began with the Stone Age, coming all the way down to the present and casting appreciative glances at Asian, African, and American developments along the way. When this mass of material proved indigestible, anthropology and ancient history were lopped off and the beginning was set at the end of the Roman Empire, with Greek cultural contributions fed in wherever they seemed most appropriate. No aspect of departmental business was given more attention than the freshman course; if chronic dissatisfaction with one's achievement was a virtue, then history was one of the most virtuous departments on campus.

And so the frugal years wore on. They were years of hand-to-mouth existence and annual deficits, of salary cuts and uncertainty about the future. Making ends meet became a fine art; the College learned to stretch the annual appropriation to cover the most urgent needs, while battling to keep classrooms and dormitories filled with qualified students. Heavy teaching schedules and burdensome committee assignments were the rule, alleviated by a varied social and cultural program. Above all, these were years of quiet inner growth.

4

Campus Life in the Depression Decade

The practices and activities to be described in this chapter were characteristic not only of the nineteen-thirties. Some of them had begun earlier, some have continued to the present day. But the focus is on the 'thirties as the time when patterns became clear and a definite image of the College emerged.

The student body at New Jersey College for Women was never homogeneous in an economic, social, or religious sense. Unlike most older women's colleges of the East, it contained few girls from the upper economic brackets, but neither did it resemble the colleges of the great metropolitan centers which were composed mainly of urban day students. The College's student population was as varied as that of the State of New Jersey, and the proportions changed in gradual response to changing population patterns of the State. It included Catholics, Jews, and all shades of Protestants. There were students from the large high schools of Newark and

Jersey City as well as from the smaller schools of the more rural western and southern regions. About 10 per cent came from outside New Jersey. In the cottages of Gibbons and of Douglass (now Corwin Campus) and the residential units of Jameson, daughters of immigrants rubbed elbows with Daughters of the American Revolution. Miscellaneous data compiled in the Registrar's office from time to time revealed the extent of the diversity. The fathers of the freshman class entering in 1927 distributed themselves occupationally as follows: merchants, 100; manufacturers and mechanics, 75; professional, 54; clerical, 28; agricultural, 20; public officials, 12. Almost ten years later, in the autumn of 1935, a study was made of the national origins of the entire student body. This disclosed that one or both parents of about one third of the 938 students were foreign-born. At about this time, too, a classroom episode revealed the variety of student backgrounds as well as interests. The members of two American history classes were asked to choose topics for term papers. One girl decided to investigate land transfers in colonial New Jersey because she had discovered, in the attic of her home, a title deed to a farm emanating from King George II and still in the family's possession; another chose to write about the Henry Street Settlement House in lower Manhattan because it was there that her mother had been welcomed and had experienced her first kind treatment in America after arriving from her native Russia.

With such a diverse student body distributed over three different residential areas on the far-flung campus, the problem of providing a satisfactory and smoothly-functioning social organization loomed larger than in other more homogeneous women's colleges and required more than cursory attention from administration, faculty, and students. Such concern had been characteristic from the earliest days on. By 1930, the structure of student government, initiated in 1923 and carefully nurtured through the remainder of the decade, was approaching vigorous maturity. While resembling that of other women's colleges in a general way, the system was by no means a blind copy of any other but was fashioned to fit the set of circumstances with which it had to deal. Its guiding principle was the conviction that the entire College, administration, faculty, and students, must be committed to the same goals and would cooperate to achieve them; hence the name: Cooperative Government Association. Familiarly known to every one on campus as "Co-op," the official name was shortened in 1942 to Government Association, or "G.A." In the words of the administrator who, more than anyone else, was responsible for its success: "There are definite and clearly defined principles [of social behavior] learned from life itself." Once these were established and kept in focus, the actual machinery of government could be changed whenever necessary to meet new situations.[1]

The main features of the system, as set up in the constitution, were the following: an association in which every one, from the Dean of the College to the lowliest freshman, held membership and had the right to vote; an elected president and vice president; an elected legislature, a small upper chamber for revision and review; and a judicial apparatus. Candidates for the top offices were nominated by a joint student-administration committee, and there was provision in the constitution for additional nominations by petition. As a rule, the candidates picked by the committee were elected, but now and then a popular petition candidate managed to upset the official slate. The names of the various governmental bodies changed from time to time, and their functions were changed or redistributed, as one College generation succeeded another, but the basic structure remained the same.

Student government was as strong as its leaders. If the president of the Association and the chairman of the Honor Board were merely popular girls anxious to please everybody, student government marked time; if they were too radical or too impatient, friction was likely to result, but little progress. But when the top posts were in the hands of capable and energetic students who had the purposes and possibilities of their office clearly in mind, things moved forward. It was such energetic leadership, for example, which in 1935 achieved student control over their own funds. Heretofore, the annual student activities fee had been paid into the general College treasury, and the College Bursar paid the bills as they fell due. But in that year the student officers requested, and received, the right to a separate budget controlled by the government association and subject only to general University regulations. They now had the full disposal of the activities fee and could allocate it to whatever purpose they wished.

In all this activity the faculty had a legitimate part, but here too the method and degree of participation varied. Originally, it was the practice of the legislature, the judicial board, and other governmental agencies to invite individual faculty members to serve as advisers. But in 1937 the constitution was amended to provide for their regular election by the students with the right to vote. The faculty opposed election by the students, insisting that if they were to be represented as a body they must themselves elect their representatives. So it was ordered and so it has been ever since.[2]

The government association had the formidable task of administering the whole body of accumulated regulations, conventions, and traditions which governed classroom conduct and campus life. Originating from student, faculty, and even University sources, these were all gathered neatly together, along with useful information of all kinds, in the student manual, the *Red Book*. The *Red Book* was an impressive document. Fed to the bewildered freshmen in humane doses and gradually absorbed by trial and error through the sophomore and junior years, it became for those seniors who had achieved a sense of social and civic responsibility an enlightening guide to the meaning of college as a whole. Few, outside the Dean's office or the ranking government association officials, managed to master it all; faculty members paid attention to it in proportion to their interest in student affairs. Yet it remained for most purposes an indispensable court of last resort.

To maintain the integrity of college life and insure acceptance of the large and complex body of rules governing classroom and dormitory behavior, an equally large and complex mass of administrative machinery gradually evolved. Its details changed from year to year but permanent and unchanging, at the heart of it, was the idea that every member individually, and the college community collectively, was responsible for keeping the procedures honest and making them work. In accepting this obligation the College committed itself to what it called the Honor System, a set of principles whose beginnings were briefly described in an earlier chapter. From 1923, the year it was initiated, to the date of this writing, the College had not departed from the Honor System. The system rested on a twofold assumption: first, that the overwhelming majority of students would accept it and live up to it out of a sense of personal honor; second, that in the rare cases of individual refusal to abide by its precepts, they, the students, would assume the responsibility to guide, admonish, and if necessary punish, the offender.

When New Jersey College for Women committed itself to this code of conduct, it was introducing no novelty. An honor system as a method of college self-government had been known in the annals of American higher education for nearly a hundred years. First to adopt it was the University of Virginia soon after its founding in 1826; a number of antebellum southern colleges followed suit. In its more sophisticated twentieth-century form it was successful in only a few of the nearly two thousand institutions of higher learning in the land, women's colleges conspicuous among these few. Probably none undertook a deeper and wider commitment than N.J.C., where from the beginning the principle was applied to academic and social life alike.

Essential to the smooth working of the Honor System, so its protagonists believed, was the requirement that every student deliberately violating a regulation be asked by anyone who knew of the violation to report herself to the proper authority within a prescribed time limit; if she failed to do so, the second party was under obligation to report the incident herself. This was the crux of the matter, the universal joint that kept the whole machinery in mesh; this was the moral absolute, the categorical imperative on which everything rested. If this foundation were withdrawn, the whole system would crumble and brave words become empty pretense. In recognition of its critical importance, the clause embodying the reporting concept was refashioned time and again as the moral atmosphere of the campus responded to the changing vicissitudes of American life. But the two steps of asking an offender to report and then doing it oneself if she refused remained intact.

However phrased, this was strong doctrine whose validity was not immediately obvious to the average New Jersey high school graduate. An elaborate program of indoctrination was therefore fashioned to make it palatable, and this had to be kept continuously up to date. The language throughout was that of persuasion and appeal rather than of harsh penalties. Yet for all the sugar-coating it was undeniable that the end of the road for the persistent transgressor was punishment, and the student who reported the offense had a hand in this punishment. For some, this was asking too much. Conflicting loyalties were involved. The larger responsibility for the good of the whole could not always stand up against those deeper-rooted instinctive fealties implied in such expressions as: it is mean to tattle, and, you don't betray a pal. The vexing dilemma continued to plague generations of students and administrators, and the issue has never been fully resolved.

Well aware of the magnitude of the problem, faculty, administration and student leaders addressed themselves courageously and incessantly to the task of gaining acceptance for a way of life which, if successful, was immensely superior to the sad old system of cops and robbers which was traditional and ingrained on most American campuses. For centuries college professors, instead of appealing to the students' sense of honor and social responsibility, had been acting on the more easily verifiable doctrine of total human depravity. Under such a regime every student was a potential cheat and miscreant to be held in leash by police methods, and every dean and professor a natural enemy to be outwitted whenever possible. Students and faculty at

N.J.C. succeeded to a marked degree in overcoming these ancient enmities and taking a stand on higher ground.

Chief credit for this success was in a large measure due to the Dean of Students, Leah Boddie. In bringing Miss Boddie to the faculty in 1926, Dean Douglass, with that uncanny instinct for personality factors, made one of her happiest choices. The person she selected for this responsible post was not a conventional product of a graduate school of education or of personnel procedure, but a successful high school teacher of history from Durham, North Carolina. Dean Boddie's first move, in collaboration with Mrs. Douglass, was the creation of a Department of Student Life. This consisted of a group of women, some young, some middle-aged, who were strategically distributed on the three dormitory campuses.[3] They were not housemothers in the old-fashioned sense, but trained counselors and administrators. College graduates themselves, with additional professional training and experience, they had faculty status and served as liaison between professors and students. Instructors with unsatisfactory students could turn to these counselors for aid in diagnosing the trouble and applying corrective measures.

Second in importance to Dean Boddie in the structure of student life was the Assistant Dean of Students, Elizabeth P. Thomas of Nashville, Tennessee. For more than twenty years these two southern ladies, so unlike in person and method, so singlehearted in purpose, fashioned a college community that had dignity and charm. Holding out at times for almost Utopian ideals, but yielding wisely when faced by inexorable social change, they exerted an influence and created an atmosphere which those who had the good fortune to live under it for four college years would long remember.

Left, Leah Boddie, Dean of Students, 1926–1951. *Right,* Elizabeth P. Thomas, Assistant Dean of Students, who worked with Dean Boddie for more than twenty years

Dean Boddie, center, with the Senior Advisers, Class of 1929

Yet all Miss Boddie's and Miss Thomas' efforts would have been in vain had they not been able to count on the willing support of the student leaders. Such leadership had to be carefully nurtured and widely distributed. The individual houses and living units on the three campuses were so numerous that a paid housemother for each was out of the question, even if such an arrangement had been considered desirable. Instead, each house was a self-governing family. This meant that each year some sixty qualified seniors had to be found, each capable of presiding over such a house and managing fifteen to thirty girls, each of whom was the proud possessor of a house key. These student house chairmen carried a heavy responsibility, for the system stood or fell with them. Few were found wanting.

Even more difficult than the role of house chairman was membership on the Judicial Board. Here students sat in judgment on their peers, and though assisted by the Dean of Students and faculty advisers, the student majority on the board was responsible for every final decision. The students chosen for this task, and especially the chairman, soon felt a chasm opening between themselves and their classmates, which was difficult to bridge. In order to maintain communication, the board had to conduct an unceasing campaign of education, explaining the positive and meliorative aspects of its work and justifying its sterner side. Shifts in student opinion as to the principal function of the Board were reflected in successive changes in its official title. Known originally as the Judicial Board, it became the Social Relations Board in 1935; ten years later the name was changed to Honor Board.

Easiest to enforce was honesty in the classroom, the so-called academic part of the system. Deliberate cheating in examinations or intentional plagiarism in term papers was intolerable and inevitably led to suspension or expulsion. On this the consensus was overwhelming. Almost equally reprehensible were bald-faced lying and brazen misrepresentation of the facts in dormitory situations. More difficult to deal with were those violations of the social code that were covered in the constitution by all-purpose elastic clauses: "willful violation of the honor system," and "conduct which brings discredit on the name of the College." Here the conflicting claims of legality and equity, of justice and mercy, were sometimes blurred, and the Board wrestled many an hour, often late into the night, to reach a decision fair to all. Whatever the Board decided, especially in borderline cases, there was likely to be opposition from segments of the student body, from friends of the accused or those not familiar with the facts. Recommendations for suspension or expulsion had to be submitted to the faculty, who almost invariably backed up the Board.

Social regulations were many and detailed, as was common in colleges for women, and their infraction provided more tedious and vexing discussions than the open-and-shut major offenses, especially when official standards varied too widely from common practice. A girl might become too exuberant at a dance or forget to greet the chaperones in the receiving line; another was guilty of unchaperoned automobiling after six in the evening; still others were noisy in chapel, or walked downtown without a hat, or ate supper at an unapproved restaurant. Most cases of this kind did not reach the court of last appeal at all, but were handled at a lower level, perhaps through a persuasive talk by the house chairman. The offenses recorded here were of the kind that present-day undergraduates would probably view with sophisticated amusement, perhaps mixed with pity for their mothers who had to submit to such a quaint Victorian regime in their college days. What Mrs. Douglass or Dean Boddie would have said about some aspects of student dress and behavior in the nineteen-sixties staggers the imagination.

Persuasion, guidance, and redirection were preferred to harsh judicial action whenever possible. The tone was evangelical, the aim to persuade the girl who was out of step to accept the mores of the community, not to punish for the sake of punishment. This "soft sell" approach occasionally met with startling consequences: a girl who had taken a drink at a dance without being seen by anybody reported herself, unasked; another who inadvertently carried a lighted cigarette into the house to answer the phone, thus technically violating the nonsmoking rule, had no rest until she reported the incident to the nearest authority. But such extreme self-castigation was exceptional.

There were formidable cases too. Not many of these dealt with classroom cheating, which remained microscopic in amount. A few random samples will illustrate their range and variety. A puzzling problem was presented by two students who, on a Rutgers fraternity week end, had allowed their escorts to inveigle them into a speakeasy (this was in Prohibition days). Their purpose, they said when brought before the Judicial Board, had not been to drink but to make sociological studies of law enforcement conditions in New Brunswick. While they were deep in their studies, the police raided the place. The Board suspended the girls until after Christmas, and voiced regrets that the real culprits, the Rutgers boys, were beyond its reach.[4] More serious was the case of the tainted election. In the voting for Cooperative Government Association offices in 1934 two juniors, one of whom expected to enter practical politics after graduation, were caught stuffing the ballot box and falsifying election returns. They were tried, convicted, and thrown out of college. None of the candidates for office was in any way involved, but as a result of the scandal the hitherto slipshod election procedures were tightened up; one long-term result was the introduction of voting machines.[5]

Life on campus was highly organized. In addition to the all-inclusive government association, every class had its officers, its meetings, its standing and ad hoc committees, and all kept records. Mute testimony to the profusion of activities were the bulging files in the basement of College Hall. The files, for example, of the annual Junior Show, an institution which flourished from the mid-twenties until it became a war casualty in 1942, included the overall report of the chairman, the reports of a dozen or more committee chairmen, copies of the musical score and of all the programs of the entire week end, plus innumerable odds and ends. An organization dinner at Cooper Hall ran to such details as the total number of cookies purchased, and the eight cigarettes, and the four yellow candles at five cents each, allotted to each table. The purpose in recording all these trivia was not, of course, to clutter the archives but to give the greatest number of students the widest possible training in the social amenities.

Clubs and societies abounded, as they did in all colleges and, for that matter, in all areas of society. Americans have always been joiners, and the N.J.C. students were good Americans. Most of the clubs were departmentally oriented, and the several departments of instruction exercised varying degrees of control over their membership and activities. Most closely integrated were the language clubs. The German Department exerted considerable pressure on its majors to insure their participation in the activities of *Der Deutsche Verein;* *Le Cercle Français* and the Spanish and Italian clubs also proved effective vehicles for familiarizing students with the culture of the country whose language and literature they were studying. Others, like the History Club, carried their department sponsorship more lightly and were by no means limited to majors. There were clubs governing nearly every field of activity, academic, vocational, athletic: Kappa Iota (*K*aptains of *I*ndustry!), Dramatic Arts, Curie Science, Crop and Spur, Pen and Brush. Their names indicate their affiliations. A number of honor societies, with membership based on proficiency and achievement, rounded out the picture; they were Delta Mu for music, Philalethean (Philo) for creative writing, Mimes for drama, Orchesis for dance.

Orchesis, honorary dance group

Clubs came and went, and while the mortality rate was not excessively high, a roster of student organizations in the middle nineteen-sixties would read differently from one of the mid-thirties. The social sciences may serve as an example of the kind of evolution that went on. In 1944, the History Club, Kappa Iota, and the League of Women Voters, sponsored respectively by history, economics, and political science, merged to form one social science club, popularly known as HEPS. This troika proved unwieldy, for it aimed in too many directions, and it eventually melted down into an International Relations Club, a more vigorous group with singleness of purpose.

The campus clubs had their social side: teas, dinners, dances, and theater parties formed an integral part of their programs. It was not difficult to find willing workers for these fringe activities, not nearly as difficult as to get contributions of high quality for the formal program. Here the pressures of class and laboratory assignments, of term papers and examinations, were usually a valid excuse for sketchy contributions to the club. Yet there was much solid work too, and some of the club papers and presentations were, intellectually, highly respectable. No doubt it all served a purpose; choosing wisely among competing values was one of the more difficult things to learn at college.

Not the least of these values was physical fitness. Sports, games, and physical exercise had received major emphasis in the early years. Students were enthusiastic then, and leading trustees made a fetish of student health. This initial enthusiasm declined somewhat in the 'thirties. For one thing, the city caught up with the campus. Competitive class hikes like those of the early years—one class rolled up a record 815 miles—were made difficult, to say the least, by super-

The YWCA Club

highways and thickening automobile traffic. Some sports were victims of the Depression. Golf and riding, with high fees, lost their popularity; the riding club, Crop and Spur, found it difficult to maintain its activities and eventually gave up the ghost. A lengthening class day and increasing pressure of studies reduced the time available for physical exercise and stirred up considerable student sentiment in opposition to compulsory gymnasium for upperclassmen. In spite of these adverse conditions, and handicapped by totally inadequate facilities, the Physical Education Department managed to provide a wide program of individual and team sports, gymnasium work, dance, and remedial physical exercise, climaxed by a public day of games, contests, and pageantry in the spring. Chief fashioners of this program over the decades were Professor Kees and her principal long-term colleagues: Virginia Ames, Wilda Long, and Dorothy Simpson.

Dances were always popular, whether sponsored by clubs or under other auspices. Barring examination periods there was hardly a week end, back in those supposedly drab Depression days, when a student could not go to a dance, formal or informal, and in some weeks she had the choice of several. There was Soph Hop in November, Christmas Formal, Junior Prom in March, Spring Formal in May, and the Senior Ball at the end of the year. There were the big Rutgers houseparty week ends, when girls moved into the vacated fraternity houses for Friday and Saturday nights, under the indulgent chaperonage of faculty wives, shuffled happily about the packed Rutgers gymnasium floor, or stood in transfixed admiration at the wizardry of Glenn Miller or Tommy Dorsey or other famous name bands of those days. For smaller dances on the home campus name bands were out of reach, but there were many minor league outfits available in the New York metropolitan area that could beat out a hot jam session or glide into a dreamy foxtrot with the best of them. Those were the great days of the American musical stage, and the current productions of George Gershwin, Cole Porter, Jerome Kern, and Vincent Youmans provided dance tunes and rhythms that have seldom been surpassed.

Music was available in quantity and quality. N.J.C. was from its earliest days "the singing college." Songs were written and tunes composed by students beginning with the class of '22 and continuing into the 'sixties. They ranged from the stately if somewhat cumbersome original *Alma Mater* to the quietly lovely and philosophical *Listen, the*

Pines and the rueful *Along With You, Pal,* kindred in spirit to the *Carmina Burana* of the wandering scholars of the Middle Ages. Class song contests on Campus Night in October and after the Sacred Path ceremony in May kept the interest alive. The Weepies, a self-perpetuating group of entertainers, furnished popular music for programs on and off the campus. For eighteen years, the Junior Show offered an outlet for members of that class to display their talents in writing the libretto and the musical score.

Musically and emotionally satisfying was the last day's program before the Christmas holidays. It began in the late afternoon, when the entire student body, dressed in white, assembled in the darkening chapel. On the stroke of five, two Yule log bearers and four torch bearers in medieval pages' costumes, all chosen because of highest academic rank, emerged to light the fire in the hearth which Mrs. Douglass had insisted on building into the chancel, using fagots made from the previous year's embers. Selected seniors, led by the president of the government association, now mounted a specially constructed stairway, lighting their candles one from the other. From here on the ritual proceeded in steady crescendo, hymns and carols alternating with the reading of the nativity story, followed by a toast, a poem, a prayer, all written by former students, to the final jubilant "Adeste Fideles." Vespers over, the procession moved, electric torches in hand, to one of the ancient pines lighted up for a Christmas tree, where more carols were sung. A special dinner at Cooper Hall followed, and the day ended with the four formal class dances, lasting far into the night.

While the spirit of the season usually carried all before it, there was an occasional sour note. In 1939, someone who called herself "Griper" announced in a letter to *Campus*

The Weepies

Members of the Class of 1930 rehearse for the Junior
Show, "S.S. Intelligentsia"

News that she was "disgusted with the enforced Christmas cheer," was not going to the dance to spend hard-earned money on a date she cared nothing about, merely because a resident counselor had lectured her on her duty to display the proper Christmas spirit.[6] There was, then, a minority point of view, but it was small and was lost in the general jubilation.

On a higher level, the professional artists of the Music Department staff contributed incessantly to the musical life of the campus. Vocal and instrumental recitals by staff members and by senior majors in the well-equipped Music Building, organ concerts and choir concerts in Voorhees Chapel, all added flavor and stature to the cultural life of the college.

Equally impressive were the contributions of the Department of Dramatic Arts, which continued to put on three public productions every year, performed by student players occasionally augmented by faculty members or by outsiders. The annual fare included plays by contemporary dramatists: Philip Barry, George Kaufman, Somerset Maugham, classics by Ibsen, and occasionally, when Mrs. Inge thought her students up to it, Shakespeare in costume. Among the high spots was a performance of Edgar Lee Masters' *Spoon River* in 1934, arranged for dramatic presentation by Professor Inge. The stage was a cemetery by moonlight seen through a gauze curtain. The characters, forty-five in all, rose behind their tombstones to deliver their lines, singly or in dialogue. Mr. Masters was there himself and gave a curtain speech during the intermission. By November of 1941 the Little Theater had reached its fiftieth production: it was James Thurber's *The Male Animal*.

There was one attempt to bring together the Music Department and the Dramatic Arts Department, in a joint production of Mozart's *The Magic Flute*. This was in 1938. Students, faculty, and faculty wives participated. A senior music major, a willowy girl with an excellent voice and considerable stage presence, played the soprano lead; a Rutgers senior handled the difficult role of Papageno superbly well. The only sour note was struck by the male lead, Prince Tamino. For this role the voice professor had insisted on bringing in a professional singer from New York. It was an unfortunate choice, for while the gentleman undoubtedly had a trained voice, he had little else to offer. Against the fresh enthusiasm of the rest of the cast his performance was jaded and mechanical; he was most unprincelike in appearance, spoke with a heavy accent, and his dual scenes with the princess were something less than convincing. The joint departmental experiment was not tried again.

Another major source of cultural enrichment was the lecture platform. Public speakers abounded, as might be expected in a college situated on the main avenue of transportation between New York and Philadelphia. Among the celebrities who spoke on the campus in the late nineteen-twenties were Vachel Lindsay, Sherwood Anderson, Edna St. Vincent Millay, and Carl Van Doren. In 1933 the government association voted to divert the one-dollar fee from the (temporarily) discontinued *Horn Book* to a lecture series, to which the faculty were also invited to contribute their dollars. The lecturers that year were the Irish poet, James Stephens, Vida Scudder, Harry Overstreet, and Edward G. Conklin. They came for honoraria, respectively, of $150, $200, $100, and $50.[7] Professor Conklin of Princeton, though a biologist of national stature, was not associated with a national lecture bureau, hence his lower fee. Such unattached

Mrs. Eleanor Roosevelt, lecturing at the College, is greeted by Dean Corwin

professors were in plentiful supply as speakers in the New York metropolitan area. Two years later, in 1935, the annual lecture series was made a continuing affair when a portion of the student general activities fee was set apart for this purpose. First speaker under the new dispensation was Will Durant, who spoke on "The Crisis in American Civilization."

Lecture evenings produced a flurry of excitement, especially among the committee in charge which usually gave the speaker a dinner beforehand, at Cooper or at Wood Lawn. Excitement ran high when the honored guest was a national figure such as, for example, Eleanor Roosevelt, who appeared on campus on three different occasions. There were embarrassing moments too. When Vincent Sheean turned up for his prelecture dinner, late and breathless, to announce that a close connection had prevented him from bringing all his dinner clothes—black tie and black shoes were missing—the professor on the committee rushed home to supply the missing items from his own wardrobe. Fortunately the shoes fit, and Mr. Sheean was able to face his audience fully clothed and in his right mind. On another occasion a packed Chapel awaited Maurice Hindus, who was to speak on Russia. But Mr. Hindus did not appear, nor was there any word from him. After nearly an hour's wait the president of government association had to step to the rostrum and announce to the assemblage that there would be no lecture that night and that they had better go home. Mr. Hindus, it turned out later, had been a blameless victim of circumstances. Soon after the Hindus episode a scheduled lecture by Lytton Strachey had to be canceled when the federal immigration authorities detained the lecturer at Ellis Island as a suspected communist. *Campus News* responded to this situation with an indignant editorial denouncing red-baiting and asking for an end to the House of Representatives' Un-American Activities Committee.[8]

Campus News was what its name indicated: the semiweekly purveyor of information about everything of importance. There were other student publications. *Quair*, an annual, presented the four-year record, with names and photographs, of the graduating class. *Horn Book*, appearing twice a year, furnished an outlet for budding poets and the handful who had the talent and the courage to attempt creative writing. But the general interest centered in *Campus*

News. With its four-page spread, sometimes augmented to six or eight, it reflected the whole of college life.

As an organ of opinion its beginnings were conservative. In its early years it faithfully reproduced the official point of view, brimmed over with loyalty to the College and its traditions, and supported the Honor System to the last dotted "i" and crossed "t." The flurry over the dropping of the political science requirement, mentioned in an earlier chapter, was a momentary aberration; it passed, and the paper returned to its traditional quest for sweetness and light.

But from about 1934 on, the climate of opinion changed. Harsh winds swept over the campus as they did over all

In 1927 *Quair*, the College yearbook, was dedicated to the State of New Jersey, represented at the banquet by Attorney General Edward J. Katzenbach. At the speakers' table are Mrs. M. Casewell Heine, active in the State Federation of Women's Clubs and an honorary member of the Class of 1928; Dr. Oral S. Coad; Dean Boddie; Dr. Sidney A. Cook; Helen Fowler, President of the Class of 1928; the Attorney General; Dean Douglass; President John Martin Thomas of Rutgers; Mrs. Cook; James Neilson; Grace McIntosh '28, Editor; and Mrs. Coad

143

America. The New Deal was beginning to take hold, but jobs were still scarce, wages low, and government regulation and aid were necessary at many points to prop up and revitalize the ailing economy. Europe meanwhile, still not fully recovered from the First World War, seemed to be repudiating the political and economic principles of democracy whose validity and ultimate triumph Americans had always taken for granted. In Italy, Mussolini was raising a police state over "the putrid corpse of democracy," and in Germany the Nazis were grinding a meek populace under an iron heel. Russia's position was equivocal: while the communist state posed as the champion of the common man against fascism, it had its own purges and tyrannies to explain, and its worldwide conspiratorial apparatus did not invite confidence in the purity of its motives. In France and elsewhere in Western Europe the communists were making common cause, for the time and for their own purposes, with the democratic forces, in what was known as the popular front; across the Channel, Tories and Laborites battled economic depression and postwar ennui, while Britain let its defenses lapse, unmindful of the rising menace on the Continent.

This confused world situation bore in on American undergraduates at a time when they were peculiarly vulnerable. Sensitive as always to changing winds of doctrine, since it was the purpose of college to examine inherited beliefs with critical honesty and new ideas with scientific objectivity, college students found it difficult in the nineteen-thirties to sustain such objectivity. For the students of that decade were beset with bread-and-butter problems as well as political confusion. It was not easy to find the money for college in the first place, and with vanished savings and unmerited unemployment a reality in their own families, the old clichés about thrift and effort and free enterprise lost some of their glamor and took on a hollow sound. Under such pressures it would not have been surprising had the idealism of the more thoughtful students and campus leaders soured into radicalism and even cynicism. A clue to the drift of student opinion was offered in a political preference poll of the senior class in 1934. In that poll the Socialist party drew the highest number of votes, the Republicans were second, the Democrats third. President Franklin D. Roosevelt was voted the greatest international figure and his Secretary of Labor, Frances Perkins, the greatest woman.

Yet radicalism in the full sense of the word remained rare at N.J.C. It had its advocates, but they were a small minority, at least in comparison with other colleges in the New York metropolitan area. But discontent was widespread, and the tepid acceptance of administration and faculty leadership in campus issues came to an end. *Campus News*, under a succession of militant and, on the whole, competent editors, led the movement toward self-assertion. These editors, history and social science majors all of them, saw in the microcosm of the campus the same forces at work as in the great world beyond, and carried the torch for a succession of changes in college life in the name of democracy, liberty, and peace.

A good opportunity to take an independent stand offered itself in the spring of 1935, when a *cause célèbre* exploded over the heads of the unsuspecting campus world. A year before, an instructor in the German department had been notified that his appointment would terminate the following June, at the close of his third one-year term. Such procedure was routine not only at N.J.C. but in American colleges generally. Instructors were temporary appointees, low men on the totem pole, with no assurance of being permanently incorporated into the faculty. It was a device to give flexibility to an otherwise too rigid staff structure. Economy was an additional factor in this case, for enrollment in German courses had dropped by about 25 per cent in the previous two years, and further shrinkage was expected. In the interest of frugal housekeeping the position itself was therefore abolished and no new instructor was appointed. But in May of 1935, a few weeks before the end of his term, the instructor unexpectedly wrote to the University Trustees protesting his dismissal and alleging that the action was motivated by the pro-Nazi sympathies of the department chairman which he, the instructor, had consistently opposed.

Now the fat was in the fire. The newspapers got hold of the story and headlines blazed from one end of New Jersey to the other, while press associations carried the item beyond the borders of the State. Then someone threw in the charge of anti-Semitism, and though this issue was irrelevant since both the chairman and the instructor were gentiles, it grew into a major sensation, and dark threats began to be voiced against N.J.C. and Rutgers, whose position as the state university was at that time none too secure. In the circumstances, President Clothier, with the consent of the trustees, ordered a full and open investigation in which all charges were to be aired. Students, faculty, and the public were encouraged to testify, newsmen were admitted, and legislative leaders invited to participate. The hearing opened in late May, and from then until the ninth of August Rutgers washed its dirty linen in public, all because the Trustees, conscious of their civic responsibility, leaned over backwards in their effort to have all the facts made public and to be fair to all sides. The investigating committee held twenty-nine sessions all told, and heard a hundred and ten witnesses.

Student opinion was divided. *Campus News*, though under administrative pressure—according to its editor—not to comment editorially, evaded the restraint by printing scores of letters from students. These in turn said little of the legal issues, on which the students were not well informed, but dealt largely with the question of pro- or anti-Nazi sentiment in the department, and with the character of its chairman. For the latter, Friederich J. Hauptmann, was himself a controversial figure. Born and educated in Germany, he was a veteran of the Kaiser's army; his teaching methods, though apparently effective, were noisy and had Prussian drillmaster overtones. In the course of the testimony, one student accused him of having thrown a book at her in class, another of hitting her over the head with a book. In rebuttal, Professor Hauptmann insisted that he had only tapped her on the head, presumably to emphasize some intricate bit of German syntax, and besides had given her a high grade at the end of the term. He insisted further that he had no anti-Semitic sentiments whatever, and emphatically denied having called Woodrow Wilson a "Schweinehund." Unfortunately, in presenting his case, the department chairman was not content to stand on his legal right under the university statutes to refuse to renew an instructor's appointment at his discretion, but maintained that in addition to everything else, the instructor was incompetent. This he found hard to prove, for there was considerable evidence to the contrary. Colleagues who had come to know the young instructor found him cultured and well-spoken, and with a wide and scholarly knowledge not only of German but of general European literature. What Hauptmann meant to charge—and the rest of the department supported him in this—was that the instructor did not willingly do the work assigned to him, that language drill in lower-level courses bored him, that he showed too little interest in his floundering students, took no part in the social activities centering at the German House, by which the department set great store, and that, as an example of his lack of interest, he had attended only one faculty meeting in three years.

After more than two months of hearings the trustees' committee published its report. This upheld the chairman against the charges of the instructor; found no evidence that the principal reason given for the latter's dismissal—shrinkage in enrollment—was not the real reason; and no convincing evidence of Nazi propaganda by the head of the department. At the same time, it chided the latter for his overly aggressive classroom tactics.[9]

A storm of protest swept through the newspapers upon publication of the report. The American Legion demanded a legislative probe, the foreign-staffed language departments were denounced, there were dire threats of cutting Rutgers funds. Many agreed with the views of a prominent citizen of New York who had earlier written to Governor Harold Hoffman of New Jersey that the N.J.C. German Department was a "hotbed of Nazi sedition" and had complained of the "tide of Naziism that seems to have saturated the institution."[10] The American Civil Liberties Union investigated and, while commending the Rutgers Trustees for their open hearings, disagreed with their conclusions. Its report, which had Reinhold Niebuhr, among others, as a signer, held that the Nazi issue had been paramount. Yet when an N.J.C. professor, happening to meet one of the ACLU investigators a few weeks later, asked him what he really thought of the case, the astonishing reply was that had he been the chairman of the German Department, he too would have dismissed the instructor.

But the last chapter in the story was still to be written. Soon after America's entry into the war in 1941, Professor Hauptmann, after abruptly asking for a leave of absence, mysteriously vanished and, though a naturalized American citizen, apparently managed to return to Germany. At any rate, a former Rutgers student in the army of occupation after the war was reported to have recognized Hauptmann as a minor Nazi functionary in a group of suspects being questioned by one of the Army denazification tribunals. His ultimate fate, though possibly recorded in the archives of the U.S. Department of Defense, has not been made public.

Although *Campus News* had played a minor role in the German Department controversy, it had encouraged comment and, by implication, taken a stand. It continued to take a stand, more frequently and more militantly, not only on campus issues, but on world affairs as these grew more urgent. International problems, the subject of lively discussion throughout these years, took on reality for the students in a variety of ways. Several European scholars, refugees from the Nazis, had found asylum on the faculty.[11] Dean Corwin was an active member of the International Association of University Women and participated in its meetings in Europe. In the summer of 1936 the Dean was caught in Spain at the outbreak of the revolution and brought home on an American cruiser, and Professor Manuel Salas of the Romance Languages Department, himself a veteran of earlier Spanish wars, had a similar narrow escape. All this caused much campus stir, which was reflected in the columns of the student newspaper and in letters from its readers. Thus an Armistice Day issue gave the entire front page, news and editorial columns, to international affairs. In another issue, some time later, the letter column was enlivened by a lengthy exchange of views between a member of the faculty, a veteran of the First World War, and the president of the government association, on the relative merits of preparedness and disarmament as a guarantee of peace.[12]

The cause of peace was close to the hearts of all students, and endless discussions, formal and informal, turned on the question of how best to secure it. There was a Peace Club conducted by Professor Emily Hickman, herself a prominent leader in a nationwide organization of that time known as the Committee on the Cause and Cure of War. The Peace Club studied world affairs, took a stand on issues, and widened its appeal by social functions such as an annual international café, complete with floor show, in which the language clubs also took part.

Campus News endorsed the aims of the Peace Club but considered its program and tactics too mild and academic to be effective. Desiring quicker results it supported, while the Peace Club regretted, such direct action projects as the peace strike of 1935. This was an event planned and directed by the American Student Union, a nation-wide organization especially strong in the colleges of the New York area. New Jersey College for Women was not affiliated with the American Student Union, but with the more conservative National Student Federation of America; individual students, however, had joined the former. The ASU planned a series of mass meetings to agitate for peace. On an April morning, according to ASU's directive to its members, students everywhere were to be induced to leave their class-rooms and assemble at some central location to hear talks for peace. The small ASU contingent at N.J.C. fell into line. Promptly at eleven, militant peace advocates flung open the doors of all classrooms and shouted: "Everybody out!" Only a corporal's guard followed the call, for it took a brave soul to get up and march out of class in the face of almost unanimous faculty disapproval; besides, majority student opinion, while sympathetic with the purpose of the strike, deplored its tactics. A year later faculty and students, to forestall a recurrence, scheduled a Chapel meeting devoted to peace; Carrie Chapman Catt was the speaker.[13]

Both national student organizations were supported by the campus paper. The small group of members of the unofficial ASU chapter included influential college leaders. They attended meetings of the National Youth Congress at which the Communist party line was regularly endorsed. There was no communist organization on campus, and there were few if any communists. Yet the editors of the paper and a wide segment of student opinion believed that Communists, like Republicans and Democrats, Christians and Jews, Negroes and whites, should be allowed to share in formulating public opinion in a democratic society. Neither they nor American college students generally were aware at that time of communist techniques of infiltration and conspiracy. "Does the House of Representatives Unamerican Activities Committee think," so ran an editorial entitled "Red, White, and Blue," that college students "cannot think for themselves and are pawns in the hands of mysterious theorists deep in the steppes of Russia?"[14]

Preoccupation with world affairs did not mean neglect of campus issues. Prominent among the latter was the question of chapel attendance and chapel conduct. Here too *Campus News* took a militantly critical stand. New Jersey College for Women was not unique in having a chapel problem. Attendance at religious services had been a contentious issue on American campuses ever since the late nineteenth century, when church and faculty controls relaxed and the inner unity of the historic liberal arts college began to disintegrate. The issue was doubly acute in publicly supported institutions like N.J.C.

From 1928 on, when Voorhees Chapel was completed, a regular Sunday service of worship had been held there, in addition to four, later two, week-day assemblies, semi-religious in character, at which attendance was compulsory. When the congregation at the Sunday services dwindled to the vanishing point, the hour was changed from eleven in the morning to the late afternoon. But these vesper services,

Choir and student body in the Chapel around 1930

Campus Night Scene

after the novelty wore off, drew no better than those in the morning, and finally in 1935 the faculty and administration took the bull by the horns, abolished Sunday services entirely except for an occasional musical vesper, and substituted a full religious service with guest preachers on Tuesdays at noon, bracketing this with a secular assembly on Fridays. At first the change met with wide approval by students and faculty alike, but then, as the restless years approached, dissatisfaction returned.

It began, mildly enough, with complaints over student behavior in the Chapel. It was difficult to force a captive audience to show respect for a performance in which many were not interested and for which they received no grades. Patiently, from one student generation to the next, social amenities committees and others concerned about the good name of the College labored to erase this blemish, but the job always had to be done over again. When on one occasion a member of the choir, which sat facing the audience, threatened to publish the names of the worst offenders, *Campus News* stepped in. The real problem, said the editor in a well-written but uncompromising statement, was not behavior, a surface symptom, but compulsory attendance. No doubt the Chapel was a beautiful building—the point of beauty and inspiration had been made—but "individual enjoyment of beauty is greatest when it is voluntary. . . . A spiritual need exists only if the individual feels this need. There can be no group need for an institutionalized religion. . . . Then we have regimentation of thought." In short, compulsory chapel was not, in the editor's opinion, sound educational policy.[15]

If the editor was looking for overwhelming agreement with her point of view, she did not get it. Letters from students and professors pointed out that an academic exercise or a campus regulation may be compulsory without ceasing to have educational value. There was for example the required freshman history course; there was the compulsory collection of the subscription for *Campus News* from all students. The paper held two polls to determine public opinion. The first came out 276–215 in favor of retaining compulsory chapel; the second, less publicized, showed 168 students and nineteen faculty in favor of retention, 78 students and six faculty against it.[16] The issue was not finally settled until 1945, when the New Jersey legislature officially declared Rutgers and all its divisions the State University and all compulsory attendance at religious exercises had to be abandoned for fear of violating the First and Fourteenth Amendments to the Federal Constitution.

On other occasions, too, the crusading newspaper failed to get its way. There was the time when the Social Relations Board suspended three students, with faculty approval. The editor fulminated: punishment had no place in an honor system; the Social Relations Board had adopted a defeatist policy, was out of touch with student opinion and might, if it persisted, kill the Honor System entirely. Dissatisfaction spread over the campus, and the government association passed a resolution requesting the board to reconsider. The latter stood its ground, refused to change its decision, and the suspensions were enforced.[17]

Another controversy came to a head in these years, over the traditional Christmas vesper service. As part of the ritual of this service it had become customary for twenty-eight seniors to mount a stairway set up for the occasion, light a series of candles and raise the highest one aloft as a signal that opened the floodgates of organ and song. For years this practice had been accepted as a dramatic moment in the celebration, but now it was found to be undemocratic. For the Dean selected these seniors for outstanding qualities of one kind or another; there were twenty-eight because the stairs had fourteen steps and only two could stand on each. No one, so the argument ran in letters and editorials, should be set apart from or placed above anyone else at Christmas time. If one had to single out a few, they should be popularly elected. And why only twenty-eight? What about the one next in line of merit who just missed the select circle, inquired one throbbing letter captioned: "That twenty-ninth girl." Dean Corwin refused to accept any change in the method of selection, but invited the students to decide whether they wanted to continue the stairs feature of the ceremony as it was or eliminate it altogether. In a college-wide referendum patronized mostly by upper class-men the vote was 273 to 235 in favor of elimination.[18] Thus the seniors-on-the-stairs part was dropped out of the vesper service. A few years later, after the war, it was reinstated at student request, but the method of selection was changed to include only the incumbents of a designated number of student offices.

The language of the paper in the turbulent years was often picturesque, sometimes abrasive. Advice to freshmen was blunt: Seek contact with minds keener and fuller than your own, even though this may be called course-grabbing by those beset with the high school ghost. Hit the books, don't procrastinate, and don't join everything the first year. "Leisurely loungers grace the campus for a short time only, and then N.J.C. gives up its dead, and another family may welcome home one who found the going too stiff." An editorial protesting a fund drive for a new gymnasium when the editor thought a new library should have priority was titled: "Hockey Balls or History Books?" The government association was described as a "company union" and compulsory chapel as "obligatory entertainment." There were references to "the spectre of the administration" which was charged with using methods "discarded by the modern democratic world." Another editorial objected to the "non-sensical notion" that college girls must appear properly dressed off campus. One issue appeared with the editorial column sensationally left blank: a front-page box explained that the space was reserved for an editorial which could not be printed even though the editors had all the damning facts.[19]

Eventually, a member of the faculty, annoyed by the constant needling, asked about the actual legal and administra-

A typical dormitory room

tive relation of *Campus News* to the college. Nobody seemed to know, and a committee was appointed to find out.[20] The committee discovered, after ten meetings, and fourteen conferences with the staff of the paper, that *Campus News* was operating in virtually complete independence of all college authority, while enjoying the free use of college space and collecting a compulsory fee from every student. The editors had unilaterally altered the constitution granted by Dean Douglass in 1928 without consulting the Dean or, apparently, anybody else. Thus the provision for a faculty adviser to be appointed by the Dean had been changed to read: "to be selected by the editor and the business manager and approved by the staff"; and the words "the editor-in-chief *shall* confer with the adviser" had become "*may* confer." In order to reestablish proper relations, the investigating committee recommended the creation of an advisory council of representatives of administration, faculty, staff of the paper, and student body.

Dean Corwin enlarged the recommendation of the committee by offering to accept any alternative proposal from the editors which would clearly recognize the responsibility of the College for its paper and would insure access to the editor for the faculty adviser. The editorial board at first refused to change its position, but when eight former editors signed a letter urging compliance as the best means of securing the freedom of expression which the board held out for, the editors reluctantly accepted the Dean's offer. Actual implementation was delayed, however, and two years later the Dean again had to remind the board of editors that they must finally conform to general college regulations regarding their officers and their budget and thus fall in line with all other student organizations. Faced with the final showdown, the board refused to comply and *Campus News* was abolished. Its valedictory editorial, on March 20, 1940, proclaimed the underlying issue as "authoritarianism . . . ever at odds with group responsibility." A year later a new student paper was organized which accepted college responsibility as outlined by the faculty committee and the Dean. It was called *Caellian,* and it brought out its first issue on February 13, 1941.

Not all was turbulence in the 'thirties. The more sensational episodes recounted here must be set in perspective against the normal routine of campus life: the lectures and discussions in scores of classrooms day after day, the hours upon hours of absorbed reading in the library and patient investigation in the laboratories, the term papers, the field trips, the preparation for examinations, all of which spelled mental growth, proceeding quietly underneath all the tumult and controversy. This too was the real College. The student leaders, whether government association officers or editors, were idealists, even the most contentious of them. But they were idealists in a hurry. They saw with clear eyes, as college students often do, the injustices and inconsistencies of a world they never made, and became impatient with what they considered the stodgy conservatism of their elders in faculty and administration. Energetic and optimistic, for all their disillusioned airs, they were romantics who hoped to see the evils of campus life and, if possible, the world brought under control before they graduated, for in the words of their song: "Great things to be done seemed simple there."

~~~ 5

War and Postwar Years

As the nineteen-thirties gave way to the 'forties and the lengthening shadows of the war in Europe drew nearer, the climate of opinion slowly changed. Disputes over campus issues grew less acrimonious. A return to older values and a drawing together for common purposes, though not fully evident until after Pearl Harbor, were clearly under way. *Caellian*, unlike the late *Campus News*, was conciliatory. When publishing complaints, the editors saw to it that an answer from the appropriate authority appeared in the same issue. When taking up the perennial issue of chapel conduct, the paper itself did not take a stand but merely invited discussion.[1] There was a general lowering of temperature and a decline of heated arguments over what had once been burning issues. So pervasive was the new era of good feeling that a much-publicized open meeting to discuss extensive proposed changes in the constitution of Government Association had to be canceled because not a single student appeared; the revised constitution was later ratified by a vote of 464 to 11.[2]

War and Postwar Years

Interest in world affairs continued at a high pitch but with little sense of direction. Hitler's invasion of Poland in September of 1939 had shattered the hopes of the Peace Club and its adherents; campus liberals were confused when the Soviet Union, that supposed bulwark of antifascism, made a pact with Nazi Germany and promptly proceeded to invade Finland and to swallow up half of Poland. The following spring the Nazi war machine overran Norway, Holland, and France, leaving Britain to see it through alone, while Japan's inexorable advance in Asia threatened America's vital interests in the Pacific. Meanwhile, in imitation of national alignments, two new organizations had been formed in the University: a committee to support the Allies, and a committee opposed to American participation in the war under any circumstances. Though the two groups engaged in some lively discussions, their clashes did not produce any deep divisions of opinion in the College for Women.

In November of 1941 the Carnegie Endowment for Peace sponsored a European diplomat for a month of lectures and discussions in the University on the theme, "Reconstruction in Europe." The lecturer was Hubertus Friedrich, Prinz zu Loewenstein-Werthein-Freudenburg, a former official in the Weimar Republic and a refugee from the Nazis. He gave about half his time to N.J.C. where his informal discussions, not only of war and diplomacy but of contrasting values and customs in European and American higher education roused general interest. He had not quite completed his allotted stay when the bombs dropped on Pearl Harbor, an event that not only entailed considerable revision of the Prince's final lectures but ushered the College into a new phase of existence. In the next issue of *Caellian* the Christmas festivities, which normally would have monopolized the front page, had to share the headlines with directives for behavior in air raids.

The war did not disrupt life at the women's college to the same degree as in the colleges for men. Student enrollment was fairly well maintained. It had crept above a thousand again in 1940, dropped to 937 in 1943, was back over a thousand by the end of the war. As for State support during these years, short rations were still the rule, though the annual appropriations did increase and faculty salaries went up a little. But new instructors were still being appointed at $1,800 a year. Some services had to be curtailed; economies of all kinds and general retrenchment were the order of the day. The University Comptroller urged faculty and students to save electricity, gas, fuel oil, water, paper, and laboratory supplies. With twenty-three of the male members of the N.J.C. faculty subject to the draft, shrinkage in the faculty roster was to be expected. Before the end of the war twenty-seven professors and instructors, men and women, had left on various kinds of war service and for varying lengths of time. Extra services were expected of those who remained. They were asked for example to teach, as need arose, in the special war-oriented University Summer Session without pay, as a contribution to the defense effort.[3] Only those escaped who left town for the summer or who obtained jobs in wartime industries.

There were other faculty losses, not directly attributable to the war. Former Acting Dean Albert E. Meder left N.J.C. after long and fruitful service to enter the University administration; he eventually became Vice-Provost and Dean of the University. Professor Frederick Burrows, who had been giving a very popular course in contemporary literature for many years, retired at the age of 77. Professor

Service men replaced college men in much of the social
life in the war years

Sidney A. Cook of psychology died suddenly in 1943. So
did Professor Earle Newton, and with him went a certain
warmth which had transformed choir concerts and all musical events.

Sustained by a common cause and threatened by a common danger, College and University drew closer together.
Students and faculty of N.J.C. took an active part in the
175th anniversary of Rutgers in 1941, a gala event which
brought such eminences to the University as playwright
Maxwell Anderson and Dean Roscoe Pound of the Harvard
Law School. As the war progressed, students were pinned,
engaged, and married to Rutgers men in increasing numbers,
for the hazards of the time stimulated early marriages and
inaugurated that long-term reversal in marriage age and

birth rate which was eventually to be characterized as the population explosion. *Caellian* started a campaign for changing the name of the college, not to Douglass, or Neilson, or Loree (all of which had been suggested) but to "The Women's College of Rutgers University." At the same time the paper maintained a sturdy independence and stood for complete autonomy of the women's college. In commenting, for example, on the temporary suspension of *Targum*, the Rutgers student newspaper, the *Caellian* editor suggested that not much was lost after all, for *Targum* was so thoroughly censored as to be no genuine student paper, while *Caellian* was free of official censorship or supervision.[4]

Curricular changes during the war were few. Dean Corwin and President Clothier returned from an emergency meeting of the Association of American Colleges with the word that the best thing women's colleges could do was to hold the line for the liberal arts, while adding such courses and activities as the emergency seemed to require. An accelerated, twelve-month academic year was not undertaken. The students were not interested: they voted down a proposal to that effect by a three-to-one majority, for most of them needed—and were needed in—summer jobs. But a variety of new courses, both academic and practical, was made available. The social science departments offered two: Democracy and its Rivals and The Organization of the Postwar World. Unfortunately, as it turned out, the postwar world paid no heed. Rutgers courses in engineering and meteorology were opened to N.J.C. students. Coeducation appeared in a small way as some Rutgers students, not eligible for military service, entered liberal arts courses whose counterparts had been discontinued on their own campus for the duration. And a wide range of extracurricular, war-oriented activities was set up in such needed skills as first aid, home nursing, nutrition, and motor mechanics. For the few students who did piece together an accelerated program, special graduation exercises were held at the end of the first semester. In keeping with the times, the speaker at the regular Commencement in June of 1943 was Mildred McAfee, commander of the WAVES; her address was broadcast over a national radio hookup from coast to coast.

A few other curricular experiments were born in wartime and died with it. A geography test, given to the entering freshman class in 1942, disclosed such abysmal depths of ignorance that the College mercifully refrained from repeating the experiment. In 1943, and again in 1944, the entire senior class took the Graduate Record Examination, designed to test the fitness of college seniors for graduate study. It came in two parts: a general test of information in the arts and sciences, and a special test in the student's major field. Faculty members asking about the nature of the test in order to judge its value were told that no one could see the questions except those taking the test. With no other recourse, several professors took the entire test along with the seniors. Their scores were revealed to no one but themselves. The compulsory feature of the Graduate Record Examination was discontinued after a two-year trial, but all seniors who expected to go on to graduate study were encouraged to take it as more and more universities required it for admission to their graduate schools.

Social activities were sharply curtailed. Club dances and similar events grew scarce; the traditional four Christmas dances were telescoped into two: one each for the two upper and the two lower classes. The freshman Hallowe'en party gave way to a defense and relief project; Dean Corwin had

A course in motor mechanics was taught by Earle G. Van Derveer, college plant foreman

Speaker at the 1943 Commencement was Mildred McAfee, Commandant of the WAVES, shown here receiving an honorary degree from President Clothier

organized a campus Committee on Defense and Relief as early as December, 1940. The most conspicuous war casualty was the Junior Show. This production, written, composed, sung and acted by members of the junior class, had been an annual event ever since the class of 1925 produced the first one in its junior year. In 1942 it was dropped as unsuitable in wartime. It has never been revived. Plans for commemorating the twenty-fifth anniversary of the College in 1943 had to be curtailed, and the celebration was reduced to one chapel program, on Founders Day. A noteworthy contribution to the anniversary was a historic volume, *Twenty-five Years*, by Rosamond Sawyer Moxon '29 and Mabel Clarke Peabody '31 with the aid of various members of the faculty and the administration. The Little Theater carried on with its three plays a year, for these were part of the dramatic arts curriculum and, besides, were considered good for morale. With Rutgers men scarce, faculty members occasionally took some of the male roles.

A new kind of entertainment, if it could be called that, appeared as the outgrowth of a money-raising project for the Committee on Defense and Relief. This was the Faculty Show, launched in the spring of 1942. It consisted of a series of skits and episodes lampooning various aspects of college life and tied to a loosely woven plot. Written, produced, and acted by members of the faculty and administration, it had roles for everybody who was willing to give the time and sacrifice a little professional dignity, from the Dean to the newest instructor. It included parodies of a gymnasium class, a freshman history class, the *Caellian* office; it presented a male group of singers impersonating the Weepies, and a botany professor in a Mae-Westish costume singing torch songs. The students, though a bit baffled at the faculty's insight into their customs and foibles, approved: the Faculty Show, they maintained, relieved tensions and made for better understanding with their professors. A second show in 1944 yielded $500 for war relief; thereafter it became a quadrennial fixture and was offered, slightly different in form and with fresh themes, in 1948 and 1952, when it cleared $1,000. In 1960 the faculty ran out of gas and there was no show, but in 1964 it was revived.

After Pearl Harbor, the Dean's Committee was enlarged and renamed the War Service Committee, and for the next four years it served, under the direction of Professor Margaret

A. Judson, as coordination agent for all war-related activities. With a membership of over twenty, drawn from administration, faculty, students, and alumnae, it became the clearinghouse for a number of active subcommittees dealing, respectively, with Red Cross affairs, community service, relief collections, lectures on war issues, and other projects, and thus brought order into the chaotic wartime enthusiasm whose momentum might otherwise have lost itself in cross-purposes. At the same time, it preserved flexibility and enlisted a maximum number of the college community in the general effort. By the end of the war its financial contribution had risen to over $16,000. This money went at first to British and Russian war relief, then to the United War Relief Chest, with

The War Service Committee of students, faculty, and alumnae, coordinated all activities related to the war. Faculty members seated are: Dr. Emily Hickman, Dr. Margaret A. Judson, and Dean Corwin. Standing: Dr. John A. Small, left center, and Dr. Eleanor B. MacLaurin, second from right

some of it earmarked for the American Friends Service Committee and similar philanthropic groups.

The educational subcommittee, under the chairmanship of Professor Hickman, not only supervised the war-oriented special courses mentioned earlier, but also sponsored bi-weekly public lectures in the severely plain, but eminently suitable auditorium on the ground floor of Botany (now Biological Sciences) Building. Thanks to the College's location near New York, and the wide acquaintance of the sub-committee's chairman, competent and informed men and women were brought to New Brunswick for these programs and the level of performance ran high. Members of the N.J.C. faculty also participated. When Eleanor Roosevelt came to speak on the duties of college women in wartime, the meeting had to be moved to Voorhees Chapel to accommodate the numbers. Reinhold Niebuhr came several times; his lucid analyses of contemporary issues were always well received. In general, the speakers were government officials, university professors, editors and publicists, and distinguished European scholars and refugees. Each speaker was asked to submit to questions and discussion after his formal address, and these were sometimes more rewarding than the lecture itself.

The War Service Committee had some useful by-products. In addition to its immediate objectives, it promoted an atmosphere of closer cooperation among all groups in the college. It gave students practice in arranging programs and managing meetings and generally increased their sense of responsibility. It directed war enthusiasms and pressures into the most useful channels, established the habit of systematic giving to the less fortunate, and broadened the education of students and faculty in world affairs.[5]

War and Postwar Years

As the tide of war receded, in 1945 and the following years, old peacetime issues reasserted themselves and new ones appeared. Dean Corwin's administration had passed the halfway mark and still had another ten years to run. Numbers increased again. The student enrollment soon climbed above 1,200, surpassing the highest figure reached at any time before, then went on to 1,300 and beyond. Administration and faculty, aware that even greater increases were impending, tried to make ready for the coming multitudes, but were hampered by the lack of space and the failure of the State legislature to provide the necessary new buildings and equipment. For immediate needs, the College was in relatively good shape. Its financial condition was excellent, according to the University Comptroller. Compared to the wartime upheavals at the men's colleges, it had been quite stable. Its schedule had not been disrupted by military requirements, nor had it been forced to accept huge numbers of veterans in the immediate postwar period with all the accompanying strain on faculty and buildings. But it was the future that gave concern.[6]

Of far-reaching importance to N.J.C., as to all of Rutgers, was a legislative act which marked another step in the long evolution that was eventually to make Rutgers the State University in the full sense of the word. In 1945 the New Jersey legislature adopted a resolution designating all of Rutgers as the State University: in response the Trustees declared that the entire institution was impressed with a public trust. Among the changes that came out of this resolution was a regularization of promotions and salary increments, as well as a pension and retirement plan, arrangements in which the women's college shared. As a result, the inequities in rank and salary under which the College had suffered all its life were now gradually wiped out, and N.J.C. professors were placed on the same levels and gathered in the same brackets as their colleagues in other parts of the University. Another consequence of the newly achieved public status was the end of compulsory chapel, for which the editors of *Campus News* had fought so lustily a decade earlier. As a state institution, N.J.C. could no longer require attendance at any religious function. Chapel services were not done away with, but henceforth students had the option of attending either the Tuesday religious service in Voorhees Chapel or a secular assembly on Friday (later changed to Thursday) in the same auditorium. This happy arrangement kept the College within the law while permitting the continued full use of the Chapel building.

The College grew more aware of University problems when President Clothier, in response to widespread postwar discontent among the faculty, established a University-wide committee on personnel procedures with a subcommittee in every college, and appointed as chairman of the whole a member of the N.J.C. faculty. While asking help with its problems, the University also proved a friend in need. When the campaign for a new college library, which had been simmering for some years, was seen to be getting nowhere, it was shelved reluctantly in favor of a student center, for which support could be expected from alumnae, other members of the college family, and special friends. The library was to come next and after that a new gymnasium. Yet in spite of heroic efforts of the alumnae, the drive for a student center also began to lag until it was incorporated into a University building program and given highest priority. Thus with Rutgers backing the Student Center was completed. It opened in 1953 as the first new building on the campus in twenty-two years. The Jameson quadrangle had been the last.

Membership in the University had its irritating moments too. Decisions of importance for the women's college were occasionally made at headquarters without prior consultation or even notification of the N.J.C. authorities. In 1954 a firm of efficiency experts swarmed over the entire University and in its final report voiced strong criticism of the College for Women, most of it, in the opinion of the College authorities, quite unwarranted. Some of the charges, together with the administration's answers, ran as follows. Charge: N.J.C. is only for highbrows, and the dropout rate is high; answer: we pride ourselves on our high scholastic standards and our dropout rate is lower than at other women's colleges. Charge: there should be a central heating system; answer: it would cost over a million dollars, which we do not have and are not likely to get. Charge: there should be a University superintendent of grounds and buildings; answer: there is one. Charge: the College should employ better-trained janitors; answer: we should love to, if they could be found. Charge: the number of student waitresses in Cooper should be reduced; answer: this is a form of scholarship aid whose reduction would cause considerable hardship. Charge: the cafeteria should be merged with the Cooper dining rooms; answer: the experts seem unaware that this is a home economics laboratory cafeteria, and instruction in that important department would be seriously crippled without it.[7]

Of some concern too was the gradual absorption by the University of certain professional and vocational departments hitherto conducted by the women's college. Three

Students crowd the library, housed in Recitation Building during the 'forties

The Student Center—later College Center—opened in 1953 as the first new building on the campus in twenty-two years

areas primarily were affected. For some years, the School of Library Science had been languishing, with fewer and fewer students; Physical Education majors too were declining in numbers; and finally the Education Department—the College had no Education majors as such—was duplicating work that could be more conveniently done by the University School of Education, especially since the latter was planning an expanded program. The University was also proposing to establish a graduate school of library service. Duplicate professional schools were unjustifiable in the eyes of the State's fiscal officers. As a result of these pressures, the N.J.C. School of Library Science was phased out, the Department of Education was incorporated in the University School of Education, and the professional part of the Physical Education Department was eventually merged with the corresponding department at Rutgers.

This absorption of professional departments, together with the growing supervision by the State, finally led to a special meeting of the Trustees' Committee in November of 1954, at which the entire position of the College in the University was to be reviewed. Such a meeting was also necessary for the orientation of the prospective new Dean, Miss Corwin having announced her intention to retire at the end of the academic year. The Associate Alumnae and the State Federation of Women's Clubs were represented and both introduced prepared statements. The faculty had expressed its views earlier.[8]

All parties agreed that the women's college had certain distinct functions which it could not perform efficiently without a secure position of autonomy within the University structure. The alumnae, after expressing their loyalty to Rutgers and to the state university concept, insisted on the continuance of the coordinate college with its separate budget, its autonomous Department of Student Life not responsible to any Rutgers dean, and the integrity of its Honor System. For the Federation, Mrs. M. Casewell Heine expressed herself in picturesque language. The Federation, she maintained, also desired autonomy with a line-item budget for the College. The women's college had been too long, like the Victorian woman, dependent upon the men in her family. Now the men in the family needed to be instructed how differently women feel about matters that have long been their concern. "We refuse the Victorian method of argument—the tyranny of tears." Nor would they stoop to political intrigue. The women of the State were proud of their college; they wanted to be proud of the University. To that end, frank discussion was necessary in a spirit of cooperation and on a basis of equality. This could be accomplished only by the greatest possible autonomy. Mrs. Alfred R. Driscoll, mother of the Governor of New Jersey, followed Mrs. Heine with an eloquent statement expressing substantially the same views.

The upshot of it all was a consensus that the integrity of the women's college must be maintained. It was generally acknowledged that communication between it and the University had occasionally broken down; the Provost's Cabinet would see to it that henceforth the lines were kept open; and Rutgers authorities expressed the conviction that past unilateral action in cases affecting the essential interests of N.J.C. had been unintentional. This sort of thing would not happen again.

Another troubling issue came to a head in the 'fifties. This one dealt with Wood Lawn, the estate left by James Neilson to the University for the use of N.J.C. alumnae.

Maintenance of buildings and grounds, according to Neilson's will, was to come out of his general bequest to the University. But by 1953 this was costing $25,000 a year, and the income from the bequest no longer sufficed to cover it. The Associate Alumnae were not affluent enough to take on the burden and asked to be relieved. A Trustees' committee, headed by Rosamond Sawyer Moxon '29, undertook to find out how Wood Lawn might "more expediently fit into the general university planning picture." It produced a plan designed to wring some income from the building. Regular noon lunches were to be served to the public, and other meals on special occasions. Additional compensation would come from the University Women's League, which agreed to use the building for its functions. The general upkeep meanwhile was henceforth to be the responsibility of the N.J.C. budget, to which the income from the Neilson bequest would be assigned. The committee's proposals were adopted, but a year's trial brought no improvement. The reasons were various. Kitchen equipment came "too little and too late"; the public lunches were inaugurated at the wrong season of the year; Wood Lawn was not centrally located and the expected customers did not come. In short, by 1955 Mr. Neilson's gift was rapidly turning into a white elephant.[9]

Rescue came from an unexpected quarter. In 1953 the College had fallen heir to a bequest of over a million dollars from the estate of Mrs. Wells P. Eagleton, a prominent civic leader who had been one of the College's founders and had served for many years on the Trustees' Committee. An active member of the League of Women Voters, Mrs. Eagleton had been interested in promoting wider participation in politics among the women of the State, and the bequest

Wood Lawn

in its original intent aimed to secure education, not only in formal political science, but in the techniques of practical politics, for the young women of New Jersey. In its final legal form, the will provided "for the advancement of learning in the field of practical political affairs and . . . actual . . . governmental processes . . . through the education of young women and men in democratic government." But— and this was where Wood Lawn came into the picture—the will did not permit the use of any of the money for buildings or any other form of capital expenditure; whatever educational arrangements were set up had to be housed in quarters provided by the College. In the absence of any other available building, Wood Lawn seemed the answer, and in 1956 it became the home of the newly created Eagleton Foundation (later to become the Eagleton Institute of Politics). A staff was assembled, the second floor was remodeled into offices and the first floor given over to lectures, seminars, and political meetings. The faculty's Red Pine Club was allowed to continue its monthly suppers there, and alumnae affairs too were still permitted; but all such activities were curtailed, for the Eagleton Foundation naturally had priority. Many of the treasures of the mansion—paintings and period furniture—went into storage, for they were no longer appropriate in the office-and-classroom atmosphere. The College and the alumnae were relieved of a vexing financial burden, but with it went a gracious tradition.

The postwar years were marked by internal growth. In her annual report for 1950–51, halfway through her last decade in office, Dean Corwin characterized these years as including, first, an expansion of community service, then wider acquaintance with international affairs, and finally a deepening of scholarship. Faculty and students cooperated to achieve these objectives. With the regularization of rank and salary and the introduction of a state-based retirement system, more able scholars could be induced to join the faculty. Entering freshman classes continued to come from the upper levels of the high schools of New Jersey: about two-thirds from the top tenth and nearly all the rest from the first quarter of the graduating classes. Various community services begun during the war continued; the lecture series on world affairs was maintained, and regular annual collections were raised for UNESCO. Student government presidents were sent to international conferences at home and abroad, while faculty members participated in such activities as the Salzburg Seminar and the international student programs of the American Friends Service Committee. Regular sabbaticals for faculty were still out of reach because of financial stringency, but the University's Research Council was beginning to be of some help here, and grants from philanthropic foundations became more numerous.

By way of making the freshman year more challenging to the better students, the faculty inaugurated a program of study known as the Freshman Seminar. A group of members of the entering class, carefully selected for interest and ability, was set to work reading notable books, classical and modern. A younger member of the History Department directed the group, assisted by colleagues from a cross section of other departments. In form, the Seminar was a series of informal meetings at which its members, student and faculty, analyzed the chosen book and used it as a point of departure for discussions that ranged widely over topics suggested by the main theme. A formal paper completed the program. The Seminar was so successful that it was extended, with some variations, into the sophomore year. One of its happiest by-products was the spontaneous formation of a second group of freshmen, made up of some who had expressed interest in the Seminar but had failed to be chosen. Calling themselves the "Sour Grapes Seminar," these girls organized a reading program entirely on their own initiative, invited some of their professors to help them, and conducted a spirited series of meetings in friendly competition with the official group.

Student interest made itself felt in other ways. The faculty had recently, after long discussion, adopted a revised statement of their philosophy of education—a Credo—and had published it in the catalogue. Soon after, the Committee on Educational Policies directed a questionaire to the students, asking their opinion, among other things, on two matters: what did the College do best, and what did it do least well. With one voice, the students replied that the Honor System was the best thing about the College. Opinions about short-comings were more widely distributed. Many students complained that the relation of the actual curriculum to the broad liberal arts philosophy proclaimed in the Credo remained nebulous to them. Just how, they wanted to know, could each particular required course be made to encourage students to think, inquire, criticize, and appreciate, instead of merely piling up a clutter of disparate facts. In a similar spirit the Student Leaders Conference in September of 1950 asked the faculty to set a faster intellectual pace.[10]

Partly under the goad of such student criticism, the faculty did some rethinking of required courses and some experimenting with new ones. Of unusual interest was The Religious Heritage of Western Civilization, offered jointly by members of the Departments of Art, English, History, Music, Philosophy, and Religion. Scientists were also drawn in, as were theologians and other specialists from the outside. Under a capable and vigorous coordinator the course flourished for several years. Then it succumbed to the difficulties that usually beset such cooperative ventures: finding an hour when all participants were free, and fitting the preparation for the course into an already full schedule of work.

The Mabel Smith Douglass Faculty Fund, established by the alumnae several years earlier for the intellectual enrichment of the faculty, had grown large enough by the mid-forties to be of some practical use. The faculty decided to bring notable scholars to campus, and the first one was Hans Kohn, European-born historian and specialist in the history of nationalism. He came for two weeks in 1947, gave a series of public lectures, led discussions of smaller groups, appeared in classes, and made himself generally available to faculty and students. After bringing in several other scholars from various fields under the same auspices in succeeding years, the faculty voted to forego the visiting lecturer and to buy educational equipment such as a microfilm reader, housed in the library and available to all.

The students of the 'forties and 'fifties occupied themselves with the usual campus interests, petty and serious, but on the whole in a tolerant and understanding spirit. The good feeling and sense of cooperation with the administration and the faculty engendered by the war years lingered on. *Caellian*, less militant than its predecessor, usually took a stance of responsibility and at times positively glowed with benevolence. It did feel obliged occasionally, in the manner of college editors, to deplore student apathy, but its own suggestions were generally constructive. It editorialized on the high privilege of attending chapel, now that the compulsion was removed. It was indulgent toward examinations and even gave way to rueful humor. As one examination period approached, a *Caellian* columnist expressed her feelings in parody: [11]

> God of all students, known of old
> Lord of the bluebook and the pen
> Into whose intellectual fold
> We come, to study now and then
> In our exams be with us yet
> Lest we forget—lest we forget!
>
> O to be in England
> Now that exams are here
> Whoever wakes in England
> Will have no cause to fear
> The molar weight or the square of logs
> The works of Heine, the theme of "The Frogs"
> In quizzes of length unsurpassed, I trow
> In England—now.

Interest in foreign affairs found a new outlet in a program known as International Week End, which came in November and was first held in 1949. It consisted of an introductory lecture in Voorhees Chapel on Friday evening by a noted contemporary international figure, followed by discussion groups on Saturday and Sunday with students and faculty participating, and a social program on Saturday evening. Foreign students in neighboring universities up and down the Atlantic seaboard were invited and came in considerable numbers. The International Week End, though quite a drain on the Government Association budget, proved an instantaneous success and became a fixture in the College program, one of the most rewarding of student-managed affairs.

Social activities multiplied again as wartime restrictions

The 1952 Christmas formal, held in the Music Building

183

International Week End was first held in 1949

were lifted, in fact they mushroomed so fast that before long curbs seemed indicated. To find out how much was going on and when the peak load occurred, the Student Life Department compiled a summary of extracurricular events in the second semester of 1953, arranged by days of the week. Another reason for the compilation was the growing pressure at this time for the elimination of all classes on Saturdays. The inquiry disclosed that in the course of that semester, not including examination week or the senior festivities at the close, there were ninety-eight meetings of all kinds that fell on Mondays, sixty-three on Tuesdays, seventy-two on Wednesdays, seventy-seven on Thursdays, fifty-nine on Fridays, eight on Saturdays, five on Sundays. Of this total, 189 were departmental club meetings, seventy-eight religious club meetings, and thirty-two Athletic As-

Lewis Webster Jones, President of Rutgers,
1951–1959

sociation affairs. In addition there were twenty-seven purely social functions, mostly dances, thirty-two off-campus occasions with late permission, and twelve week-end trips to conferences in other cities, in which eighty students were involved.[12]

Objection to classes on Saturday mornings—there were no Saturday afternoon classes—was growing more frequent. Almost from the beginning, the scheduling of classes at N.J.C. had been arranged in two alternating blocks of courses each meeting for fifty minutes three times a week, the one group on Mondays, Wednesdays, and Fridays, the other on Tuesdays, Thursdays, and Saturdays, with laboratory sessions attached to one or the other. This symmetrical division of the week's work provided a quantitative norm for all courses and simplified the arithmetic for computing graduation credit. But this schedule became increasingly difficult to maintain because it ran counter to prevailing trends. The business world was shortening its work week because of automation and increased efficiency, and Saturday was more and more becoming a holiday in factory and shop. With the confirmation of Rutgers as The State University in 1945, its personnel were declared public employes and as a consequence all College and University offices closed on Saturdays to conform to the practice of state offices in general. Pressure rose, from faculty and students, to close classrooms as well. Besides, New Jersey was a small state and the incentive to go home for the week end was strong. When the students, speaking through their curriculum committee, asked to have Saturday classes abolished, Dean Corwin appointed a faculty committee to investigate. This committee, after carefully examining the situation, recommended that they be retained. It did so largely because of representations made that the entire continuity of campus life and all values associated with it would be jeopardized if Saturday became a free day. Under the committee's urging, a reluctant faculty voted by a narrow margin to hold the line for Saturday classes. It was an unpopular decision. These classes continued to be eroded by unilateral departmental action until they were finally abolished in 1958, when a standardized five-day class schedule was put in force throughout the University.

A related question was that of class attendance in general, a thorny issue here as in most American colleges. At N.J.C. the practice was essentially as follows. Every instructor had virtual autonomy in dealing with attendance in his classes, except that he was expected to keep records and to report three successive absences to the Dean of Students. If at the end of the term an instructor considered a student's absences excessive, he could recommend to the faculty, via a screening committee, that her credit for the course be reduced by one or more points. This could be embarrassing to the student in that it endangered her chances of graduating with her class. There was a further faculty ruling that absences on the day before and the day after every college holiday be fined at the rate of two dollars for every class missed. Whatever the philosophy underlying it, this little device worked marvelously well; the students detested it but they came to class. In 1951 the Government Association Assembly petitioned the faculty for abolition of this apparatus and the substitution of unlimited cuts. If granted, this would have meant that the student assumed full responsibility for coming to class or staying away; she might fail the course if she cut too often, but would no longer be fined or subjected to a reduction of graduation credit. The faculty denied the request, saying in effect that an American undergraduate campus college was not the same as a European university.[13] But here, too, as in the case of Saturday classes, time was on the side of the petitioners. By 1963 preholiday fines and, by 1964 the docking of course credit, had been abolished.

Student relations with Rutgers were cordial. Rutgers items found their way into the college paper to a greater degree than in earlier years. In one year, 1947–48, the pages of *Caellian* were opened to a heavily humorous and patronizing column by two Rutgers students who called themselves the Scarlet Pixies. One issue in the autumn of 1952 gave over almost the entire front page to an all-University boat ride and the football game with Princeton, with pictures of the cheerleaders from N.J.C. Students were of two minds about girl cheerleaders: while some welcomed the innovation as a sign of healthy college spirit, most upperclassmen opposed such manifestations of delayed adolescence, believing that college students should have outgrown such juvenilia by the end of high school. For a while the students contributed to the upkeep of the Rutgers student radio station, WRSU, and on one occasion they invested $100 in the production of the Rutgers show: *Boys in Ivy*. This was a rueful experience, for the expected profit turned out to be a deficit and only $70 came back into the treasury. When at another time a *Targum* article had, in the opinion of the students, distorted the Honor System and insinuated that the girls did not really want it, the president of Government Association wrote a reply to *Targum* patiently explaining the honor code and the idea of collective responsibility behind it.[14]

The Honor System was subject to the same continual reexamination and overhauling as before the war, but there

WRSU, the Rutgers student radio station, provided one coeducational activity

was virtually no opposition to the idea itself. Students and faculty were committed to it; the Honor Board, the Student Life Department, and others were constantly at pains to explain it. On a less exalted level, the daily routine of campus life produced occasional annoyances, many of them minor. *Caellian* usually published the complaints along with the administration's answers. A sampling of these petty peeves included items like the following. There was some to-do about coming in at midnight on Friday instead of eleven-thirty. To the question as to why was there no smoking room on College Hall Campus came the answer that no room was available, for all were in use for other purposes. When students asked for brighter lights in their dormitory rooms, the Bursar replied that they could have them if they were willing to give up their electric hot plates, hair dryers, radios, and record players. The houses, he pointed out, were not adequately wired to carry the full load. And to the perennial question why certain dishes were not placed on the menu at Cooper came the standard answer that they had been served in the past until the students demanded that they be removed. Food fashions and menu preferences seemed to run in cycles.[15]

Neither Government Association nor *Caellian* took any extreme position on public affairs but preserved, on the whole, an attitude of good-natured reasonableness. The newspaper, it was true, frequently complained of lack of student interest, yet at the same time it expressed disgust, early in the election year 1948, at the extreme and sensational propaganda of the Students for Wallace group. On one issue the students did take a decided stand, and that was when three members of the Rutgers faculty refused to answer certain questions of the U.S. House of Representatives Un-American Activities Committee regarding alleged former Communist affiliations. In statements to the University authorities the three men had disavowed present membership. Nonetheless, they were dismissed from the faculty. Government Association wrote a letter of protest to the President of the University and *Caellian* protested similarly. They took the position that a professor, like any other citizen, was entitled to stand on his constitutional rights and refuse to answer questions by a Congressional committee if he feared that by answering he might lay himself open to malicious charges that could incriminate him. This, they believed, had nothing to do with a person's qualifications as professor or research specialist. "Taking the Fifth is not proof of unfitness to teach." [16] This was substantially the position taken by a faculty committee appointed by Presi-

dent Jones to express a judgment about their three colleagues.

A student poll disclosed 62 per cent opposed to the dismissal of the professors. The percentage was a good deal
higher among the upperclassmen, lowest in the freshman
class. Apparently the students were learning *something* in
college. The *Caellian* editorial commenting on the vote
began: "If you are blasé about McCarthy and what he
stands for, don't read any further," then went on to complain about the small total vote, only 280 in a student body
of over 1,300, as proof of the fear which Senator Joseph
McCarthy of Wisconsin had cast over N.J.C. as over American colleges generally. A later editorial was more hopeful:
even at N.J.C., it pointed out, there was increasing awareness of the situation, and opposition to McCarthy was growing. It was to be hoped that the rising tide of resentment

A Government Association meeting in 1953

would soon engulf him.[17] Yet *Caellian* sadly admitted that the whole controversy over the Rutgers professors and the larger issue of McCarthyism had not provoked a single letter to the editor. Whether out of ignorance or apathy or fear, the students remained unresponsive. Yet interest and concern were not entirely lacking. When a faculty panel made up of members of the English, German, History, and Political Science Departments, with a sociologist as moderator, was prevailed upon to discuss the entire issue in a public meeting, the assembly room in Agora was filled to overflowing. Even so, students claimed that they had asked thirty professors before they found five willing to undertake the thankless task.[18]

The early nineteen-fifties marked the end of an era. A number of people who had given the College definite form

Members of the Queens Theatre Guild in a scene from "The Heiress" in 1953

Sacred Path ceremony in the late 'forties

and character retired in these years. Furthermore, a change in the name of the College was impending, as well as a fundamental change in the University charter. Clearly, a chapter was closing.

In June of 1951 Dean of Students Leah Boddie and Assistant Dean of Students Elizabeth P. Thomas retired. Between them they had established the Department of Student Life and put the stamp of their personalities on the character of the College. The system they had built continued to function but under new leadership and inevitably with different emphasis. A year before, Professor Jane Inge had given up her chairmanship of the Dramatic Arts Department, and with her went the unique touch that she had given the productions at the Little Theater ever since her arrival in 1926. The Dramatic Arts Department continued to flourish; in fact it expanded to absorb the Rutgers Queens Players and become the lively center of dramatic instruction and activity for the entire University. But here too the flavor was different. Then, in 1952, President Clothier of Rutgers retired after nineteen years in office, during which he had carried the University through the lean years of Depression and the hectic days of war. He was generally popular at the women's college for his appreciation of its needs and his' efforts, within the limitations set by circumstances, to meet them. His going marked the end of the old Rutgers.

Finally, in 1955, Dean Corwin relinquished the helm which she had held, through fair weather and foul, for twenty-one years. No colorful leader like Mrs. Douglass, and congenitally averse to flamboyant self-assertion when presenting the cause of her College before the authorities of University and State, Miss Corwin remained throughout a rational exponent of the liberal arts. In her final report to the Trustees, she saw their liberating values persisting through Depression, war, and postwar expansion. In the future as in the past, the world would need college graduates who possessed not only skill and information but character and ideals, which in turn were transmitted by great teachers. On this note, personal communication and the influence of teacher on student, she closed her professional career. In a resolution of appreciation the faculty paid tribute to her level-headed guidance and selfless devotion, her lack of dictatorial qualities, and her loyalty to the University without any forfeit of cherished autonomy. On the human side, the resolution mentioned her informal cordiality as hostess and as guest, as well as her ready calls of sympathy and help to colleagues in sorrow or distress. And so, with the retirement of Dean Corwin, Dean Boddie and Dean Thomas, and President Clothier, the old order ended.

~~~ 6

From N.J.C. to Douglass

In 1955, after years of agitation to this end, the College changed its name to Douglass. The original name, New Jersey College for Women, was historically correct, for the institution had been established to serve the young women of that state. Shortened to N.J.C., the name had picked up considerable sentimental appeal through the years, and students and alumnae could become quite emotional over those three little letters. But it was a long name, an awkward name, and was constantly being confused with teachers colleges, junior colleges, and other state institutions. Its association with Rutgers made it particularly cumbersome. As one unsentimental critic put it: one could die for dear old Rutgers, but who would want to die for dear old New Jersey College for Women—the Women's College of Rutgers University—The State University of New Jersey? Other women's colleges were named after their founders, why not give this one a similar identity? And so the pressure was built up until in April of 1954 the Trustees' Committee recommended the change; the University Board approved and authorized the College to take the necessary steps to make it effective. A student poll meanwhile had come out 85 per cent in favor of the new name, and the Board of Directors of the Associate Alumnae, following an earlier poll of all graduates, likewise voted for the change.[1]

Preparations took a year. A committee headed by Dean Corwin and including representatives of the faculty, administration, students, and alumnae, was in charge. Under the astute direction of Frances E. Riche '32, Secretary of the College, all the multitudinous details were successfully attended to, and all was ready for the change-over by Founders Day, April 16, 1955. The night before, a hilarious get-together of students, faculty, and administration commemorated the passing of N.J.C. with skits and songs. A glamorized Professor Jessie Fiske belted out "Big Bad Bill," and the faculty "Weepies" sang disconsolately, to the tune of "Along with You, Pal":

> Tonight we still are N.J.C.
> Tomorrow Douglass we must be.
> We love the old, we like the new
> Oh gee! Oh gosh! What shall we do?
> We're schizophrenic.

The next day, at a formal convocation in Voorhees Chapel, Frederick W. Smith, chairman of the Trustees' Committee on the College for Women, announced: "It is now declared and proclaimed that the name of this institution, known heretofore as the New Jersey College for Women, is changed and henceforth it shall be known as Douglass College." [2] With the exception of a few unreconciled alumnae who insisted that their college was and always would be N.J.C., the change of name met with general approval.

From N.J.C. to Douglass

The Weepies singing in Cooper Hall, following Dean Corwin's announcement that the name of the College would be changed from N.J.C. to Douglass

The Faculty Weepies sang at a party the night before the name-change Convocation. Seated: Dr. Roger S. Sweet and Chester Snedeker. Standing: Dr. George P. Schmidt, Robert M. Walter, and Dr. Thomas Weber

As the old era came to a close, the College could look back on thirty-seven years of purposeful activity. True, it was not noted for any radical educational innovations, nor had it gained the prestige that age and selectivity had given to some other women's colleges; but it had acquired certain distinguishing characteristics and was not "just another college." In retrospect, four achievements in particular seemed to stand out. They were, first, its conspicuous success in welding a heterogeneous mass of girls, differing widely in economic, social, racial, and religious background, into a homogeneous society with good manners and high ethical standards; then the achievement of collective responsibility of the entire college community resting upon the premise of personal honor; in the third place, a faculty which took its obligations seriously, was never a rubber stamp to any dean or president, set high academic standards and made the welfare of its students its first concern; and finally, an alumnae association which, in the words of a contemporary observer, was "fantastically loyal" to its alma mater. These were the things that had made N.J.C. the kind of college it was.

A year after the name change another legal reorganization took place with far-reaching consequences for Douglass, as for the whole University. In 1956 Rutgers passed finally under the control of the State of New Jersey when, with judicial sanction, the Trustees adopted, and the legislature approved, an amendment to the old colonial charter. This amendment created a new controlling body, the Board of Governors, which was superior to the Trustees and the majority of whose members were appointed by the Governor. Thus Rutgers—and this included the College for Women—became a public corporation, the State University in the full sense of the word.

The name-change Convocation was held on Founders Day, 1955. President
Lewis Webster Jones leaves the Chapel with Governor Robert B. Meyner

Douglass College: A History

The changes in name and status coincided with a new administrative regime. For months before Dean Corwin's retirement at the end of the academic year in 1955, the Trustees had been busy with the choice of a successor. In contrast to their procedure when Dean Douglass retired, they took the faculty into their confidence. An elected faculty committee worked closely with the Trustees' committee, met and interviewed every seriously considered candidate, and declared itself fully satisfied with the final choice. The candidate chosen was Mrs. Mary Ingraham Bunting, a geneticist from Yale, widow of a professor of the School of Medicine, and the mother of four children. Born in Brooklyn, Mrs. Bunting was an alumna of Vassar and had earned her Ph.D. at the University of Wisconsin. Her coming added a new dimension to campus life. There had been no children in the Dean's house in thirty years, not since the early days of Mrs. Douglass.

The new Dean of the College moved into the situation with vigor and enthusiasm. She realized that the change to a full state university marked the beginning of an era with new responsibilities and new opportunities. "Douglass College," she explained in her first annual report, "is in process of evolving from a relatively small, relatively isolated, college for women to a large, well-integrated organ of the State of New Jersey." [3] In all her meetings with the Trustees and with the faculty she hammered away at the theme: the College *must* expand to meet the needs of the young women of New Jersey. Statistics bolstered her argument. If Douglass were to do no more than continue to enroll its existing proportion—2.1 per cent—of the girls in the senior high school classes of the State, it would have at least three thousand students by 1968.

Mary Ingraham Bunting, Dean of the College, 1955–
1960, with her children, the first in the Dean's house
in thirty years

This meant, first of all, a comprehensive building program, both of classroom space and dormitories. Construction of the former was facilitated by a publicly approved (1959) bond issue of $29 million for capital expenditure in the State University, with Douglass College sharing in the priorities. Dormitories could be erected with the aid of self-liquidating loans from the federal government. Compared with the lean decades of the immediate past, this was munificence. For the next eight years, continuing through the whole of Dean Bunting's administration and into that of her successor, the building program proceeded at such a rate that one could, by the mid-nineteen-sixties, speak without exaggeration of the new Douglass College. Living quarters came first. Between 1959 and 1963 there arose, in the area beyond Wood Lawn and bordering the grounds of the College of Agriculture, four new residence halls: Woodbury, Nicholas, Lippincott, and Katzenbach, designed for 250 students each, and a new dining hall to serve them. Known collectively as Neilson Campus, this new aggregation of buildings took its place alongside the already existing dormitory groups: Corwin,[4] Gibbons, and Jameson.

Highest priority among the academic structures was given to a new library, which was sorely needed to replace the crowded makeshift in the Arts Building. For years, faculty committees had planned for such a building, but nothing had come of their efforts; now, thanks to a $1 million appropriation by the State Legislature in 1958, supplemented by $75,000 given by alumnae and friends over the years, hopes were realized. In the spring of 1961 the new Library-Study Center was dedicated. Centrally placed, flanking the Chapel, the Library was a well-designed building with light and space, and plenty of room to expand beyond the 133,592

Neilson Dining Hall

volumes that were brought over from the old quarters. It was a credit to the College and received favorable notice in architectural circles.

The instructional buildings accruing from the bond issue of 1959 were one for home economics and psychology, and the first stage of a new gymnasium. The Home Economics Department had long outgrown its cramped quarters in Science Building; its equipment was obsolete and inferior to that of the better high schools of the state. Even so, financial exigencies forced the home economics people to share their new building with the psychologists. The Psychology Department had long been nomadic. From 1947 on its members had their offices with the social scientists in Carpender Hall, an old residence made over into faculty offices, while their laboratories were set up wherever space could be found. One such space was the basement of Carpender, where they set up experiments with white rats. The old mansion was not designed for such exotic activities; ventilation was nonexistent and the history professors on the first floor complained bitterly when the zoological fumes from the rat cages oozed into their offices. Understandably, the psychologists wanted out. Here were the makings of a compromise. One building was erected, with state and some federal money, to house both home economics and psychology. It was a marriage of convenience—the Dean called it a shotgun wedding—but both departments found themselves, in September of 1963, in expanded modern surroundings where they could carry on in a manner befitting members of a self-respecting college in a state university. (In 1966 the building was named in memory of Margaret Brouwer Davison, a former resident of Englewood, New Jersey, who was a benefactor of the College.)

Library-Study Center, dedicated in 1961

Loree Gymnasium, the first unit of which opened in 1961

Earlier in 1963, the first unit of the new Loree Gymnasium was opened. Appropriately named after the more-or-less benevolent despot of the College's early years, it furnished at least partial relief from the packing-box monstrosity in which all physical education had been carried on for the past forty years.

Last of the academic structures completed at this time was a classroom and office building for the liberal arts: Emily Gregory Hickman Hall, which was opened in the fall of 1964. Standing in the curve of George Street on the site of the old riding ring, this commanding six-story building became the new focus of the campus complex. Its thirty-two classrooms and two lecture halls seating three hundred and five hundred respectively took the pressure off the old classroom buildings, while the upper stories provided modern offices accommodating seventy faculty members. With awe and wonder the professors of English, History, Political Science, and Philosophy emerged from the seedy comfort of their old quarters to the gleaming efficiency of a new home, complete with automatic elevators and sweeping views of the surrounding countryside.

But while the gains were obvious, some of the old informality was lost. Geographic location and territorial propinquity of offices and classrooms had exercised a subtle influence on faculty relations and efficiency. Carpender Hall, the Victorian mansion at the heart of the campus, was a case in point. The central lobby, with its enormous threadbare oriental rug of uncertain age, was the domain of the building's only secretary, who served all the departments housed there. Student assistants shared this realm with her. Radiating from the lobby were the offices of the history

Hickman Hall

and political science personnel, with the chairman ensconced in the walnut-paneled gun room. Toward the rear, in what had been the kitchen, Professor Shirley Smith conducted the Classics Department, storing her lantern slides in the cavernous fireplace. A wide open stairway led to the Economics and Sociology offices on the second floor; Psychology, also housed there, spilled over into the servants' wing. And on the top floor the philosophers held sway; from their windows in the cupola they could survey the distant scene and keep everything below in perspective. In such gregarious surroundings contacts between departments were informal and casual; dropping in on a colleague for a chat or running into him on the stairs saved hours of formally scheduled meetings. In this way interdepartmental projects were hatched and difficulties ironed out to a degree that no amount of administrative machinery or directives could have achieved. By contrast, the new offices in Hickman Hall, though far superior in comforts and equipment, did not lend themselves to this easy interchange. There each department, isolated on its own floor and much larger than in earlier years, tended to become self-sufficient, and contacts with colleagues of other departments narrowed down to passing the time of day in the elevators.

The architecture of these new buildings was no longer Georgian but, for want of a more precise term, "modern." The last Georgian building on the Douglass campus had been the Student Center. The historic style, with its hipped roofs and white stone ornamentations, was proving too expensive; the severe new mode on the other hand was the delight of budget directors and legislative appropriation committees: you got more for your money. Besides, architecture, like all the arts, was moving inevitably toward new

Room in a dormitory on Neilson Campus

forms, and it would have been difficult to find a reputable architect willing to design anything in a style considered outmoded. By and large, the new structures were superior to their predecessors in equipment and convenience. The first students housed in Woodbury Hall on the new Neilson Campus were so overwhelmed with the luxury of their new surroundings when compared with Gibbons or Corwin that they facetiously called their dormitory the Woodbury-Hilton. As for beauty of design, opinions differed, though there seemed to be some agreement that Hickman Hall, the only high-rise structure, was the right building in the right place. Beautiful or not, it was a different campus as some of the wide expanses of open land were taken up by buildings. On the northern border of the College's domain the town closed in. Formerly the classroom buildings there had offered a long view of downtown New Brunswick, the Raritan, and the Watchung hills beyond; now this view was largely blocked by a high-rise apartment building.

The new buildings were soon filled with students; in fact the applications for admission ran far beyond the capacity even of the new facilities. Enrollment had leveled off at about 1,300 in Dean Corwin's last year because of lack of space, but now it advanced in giant steps and doubled in ten years. Costs meanwhile increased moderately. Tuition, after being calculated on a credit-hour basis for a number of years, was again fixed at a flat annual rate, now $400 for New Jersey residents, $100 (later raised to $236) more for students from outside the State. Overall costs to New Jersey residents were estimated by college authorities as averaging $1,700, a figure that was raised in 1966 to $1,900.

With all the increase in numbers there was no relaxing of standards. Applicants were screened as carefully as ever. True, the personal interview had to be given up because of the pressure of numbers, and was henceforth required only of scholarship competitors. But the entering classes continued to represent the cream of New Jersey high school seniors. Consistently, year after year, about four-fifths of the freshmen came from the highest tenth of their graduating classes. The maintenance of standards was not made easy by the state authorities, who insisted that the traditional student-teacher ratio of about ten to one be increased to over twelve to one, thus bringing it into line with the rest of the university. This meant larger classes, the merging of sections, the substitution of lectures for discussion groups, all of which required greater efforts and ingenuity on the part of the faculty if a high level of teaching effectiveness was to be maintained. In the opinion of the evaluation team

Ravine Bridge in the late 'fifties

of the Middle States Association of Colleges, which surveyed the entire University in 1956, they were meeting the
challenge. "The faculty of Douglass College," said the Middle States' report, "should be commended for their deep concern with teaching, the high standards they have maintained,
and their vigorous and responsible leadership in educational
matters." [5]

Standards were raised in other ways. Under Dean Bunting's
prodding, a systematic attempt was made to interest students
in further study after graduation. They were urged to take
advantage of the growing numbers of graduate scholarships
and fellowships available to seniors doing distinguished
work. The campaign got results. In three years, the number
of Douglass seniors going on to graduate study rose from
4 to 17 per cent.[6] Another of the Dean's projects was the
opening of the College doors to young and middle-aged

women who had dropped out before graduation to marry and raise families, and were now ready to return to some convenient college on a part-time basis to complete their degree programs. Many such were living in New Jersey communities accessible to Douglass. The faculty relaxed the rules sufficiently to enable them to enter and was rewarded with a substantial number of capable and interesting students.

An administrative innovation, approved by the faculty in 1956, was the College Council, made up of five professors (later eight) and three deans. Members of the faculty had been chronically overburdened with committee work, and the Council, which replaced three of the most important

The College Council, instituted by Dean Bunting in 1960. Seated: Dean Bunting, Dr. Eleanor B. MacLaurin, Dr. Fadlou A. Shehadi, Dean of Students Marjorie M. Trayes, Dr. Edna R. Sostman '43. Standing: Robert G. Bradshaw, Barbara J. Wells, Dr. Jacques Fontanet, Assistant Dean of the College Edna M. Newby '31, and Dr. Neil A. McDonald

standing committees, represented an attempt to do three things: to reduce the committee burden, to coordinate the work of a number of parallel committees each of which saw only one aspect of the College's problems, and to concentrate important decisions in one central agency. Members of the Council were relieved of some other duties and were served by a full-time Executive Secretary. After some initial fumbling, the Council worked well and was continued at the end of a three-year trial period with an overwhelming vote of confidence.[7]

In the midst of all these activities Dean Bunting resigned her office, having given the College four years of energetic leadership. Elected to the presidency of Radcliffe College as of February 1, 1960, she retained certain responsibilities at Douglass until April 30. John L. Swink, then Dean of Administration, and now Vice President and Treasurer of the University, served as chief administrator of the College for the remainder of the academic year.

Forward-looking and always open to new ideas, Mrs. Bunting came to Douglass at the right time and, like the proverbial new broom, swept out many a musty corner. Never hesitating to question precedents and traditions that had outworn their usefulness, she at the same time created new traditions; an instance, not profoundly important but characteristic, was her attempt to lighten solemn faculty meetings by prefacing them with coffee and cookies. She sparkled with ideas and projects, not all of which were translated into workable programs. Her methods were informal, and protocol was never allowed to interfere with desired objectives. But she was not dictatorial; she used the machinery of the faculty Council to the full, both as a

John L. Swink

sounding board for her ideas and as a source of advice and criticism. She and her children were popular with the students. The faculty liked her and, except for a few traditionalists, approved her overall objectives. She typified the transition from N.J.C. to Douglass.

7

The Fifth Decade

To succeed Dean Bunting the Trustees, again with the aid of a faculty and an alumnae committee, chose another scholar, this time from the humanities. Ruth Marie Adams was professor of English at the University of Rochester when chosen Dean of Douglass as of July 1, 1960. A native of New York City, she had graduated from Adelphi College and earned her Ph.D. at Radcliffe.

The College Hall staff with which the new Dean was to work contained some new faces. Marjorie M. Trayes, who after several years as Counselor in Residence had succeeded Leah Boddie in 1951 as Dean of Students, addressed herself to the formidable task of guiding, in an age of rapidly changing values, more than twice as many students as Dean Boddie had ever had to contend with. Roberta F. Powers had taken over the growing complexities of the Registrar's office, and Clyde F. McAlister, who had been Assistant Bursar for two years, succeeded the late Chester W. Snedeker in the sensitive post of Business Manager.

Two alumnae meanwhile had moved into positions of im-

Ruth Marie Adams, Dean of the College, 1960–1966

portance in College Hall. When in 1956 the office of Assistant Dean of the College was created, Dean Bunting appointed Edna M. Newby '31 to the post. With the exception of Rosamond Sawyer Moxon '29, a charter trustee of Rutgers and a member of the Board of Governors, Miss Newby was the first alumna to reach such a high rank in the administrative hierarchy. She had served Douglass in one capacity or another ever since her graduation, only taking time out to be a U.S.O. director for three years during the second world war. Thoroughly familiar with administrative processes and problems, she also understood the position of the College in the University. Always ready to take on extra assignments, she had earned the respect and regard of the faculty, and her appointment as Assistant Dean met with general approval. "I would hate to try to run the college without her" was Dean Adams' verdict on her second in command.[1] Frances E. Riche '32 joined the staff of the Associate Alumnae after several years as a high school teacher of English, became Executive Secretary and also served as Editor of the *Alumnae Bulletin*. In her dual role she raised the effectiveness and the prestige of both. In 1951 she assumed the difficult and many-faceted position of Secretary of the College, and soon made herself indispensable. Both Miss Newby and Miss Riche brought to their long association with the College a loyalty that few could match and a sense of perspective that grew with each year of service.

Supported by a cast of this quality, the Adams administration got under way. Even more than that of Dean Bunting, it was marked by rapid growth, expanding functions, and increasing organization complications. Student enrollment, which had been 1,079 when Dean Corwin retired in 1955, had reached 1,731 in 1960, and mounted to 2,844 by 1967.

The corresponding figures for the faculty were 125, 168, and 231. The building program of the Bunting administration was brought to completion and several new projects were undertaken.

An addition to the Student Center, now renamed College Center, doubled its size. Main purpose of the addition, opened in the fall of 1966, was to provide a campus home for the commuting students, now numbering over six hundred, who had been crowded out of their forty-year-old Beehive by the expanding needs of the Chemistry and the Bacteriology Departments. The addition also provided food services, including a dining room especially for commuters and another for the faculty. Built in the "modern" style, it attached itself to the stately Georgian original like a jeep hitched to a coach-and-four. But it was a serviceable wing, and its interior was most attractive.

Corwin Campus, after long and justifiable agitation by its inhabitants, was modernized and refurnished. But the Gibbons residences were declared expendable and plans were drawn for a new complex of residential units on that campus, which would, however, preserve the principle of small separate living groups as far as finances permitted. And time was running out on venerable Cooper Hall. Eventually Jameson Campus would have to be enlarged and a new classroom-office building provided if the undergraduate body was to grow to 3,500 as projected.

Of major concern to the College in the 'sixties was the proposed reconstruction of the New Brunswick components of the University and the place of Douglass in the new structure. Rutgers, like state universities elsewhere, was under mounting pressure from the citizens of the State to make room for their sons and daughters who aspired to a college education. Existing buildings, equipment, and faculty were totally inadequate to take care of the thousands already thronging the high schools of the State who would soon be clamoring for admission. By 1975, it was estimated, the University would have to provide for 25,000 day students in addition to all its other functions. To meet these needs without any lowering of academic and professional standards required the most careful and far-sighted planning. Well aware of the magnitude of the problem, University authorities under the leadership of President Mason W. Gross were reexamining the existing organization and services with a view to making the University over into a fitter instrument for meeting the higher education needs of New Jersey.

The plan for reorganization under consideration as this book goes to press was drafted by the Provost's Planning Committee in 1967 and called the Federated College Plan of Organization for the Residential Colleges in the New Brunswick Area. Its aim was to provide unity with diversity by setting up University-wide academic disciplines and faculty membership together with a series of separate and distinctive undergraduate colleges of manageable size. The first would insure the highest quality of teaching and research, the second would avoid the creation of a monstrous administrative monolith incapable of effective control. In this proposed new scheme of organization Douglass, as the University's college for women, would have an integral role, as would the men's colleges in New Brunswick. At least three new colleges, all coeducational and each with an enrollment of 3,500, ultimately would be built on land, formerly Camp Kilmer, acquired from the Federal Government. The first of these, Livingston College, was projected for opening in September of 1969. The new colleges and Douglass were

Mason Welch Gross, President of Rutgers,
The State University, 1959—

each to be "small enough to be an intellectual community in which students and Faculty can feel at home, and small enough for the Faculty to be able to think of the students not as decks of IBM cards but as individuals . . ." [2]

As proposals for reorganization of the University emerged, such as the Federated College Plan, doubt and concern about the future gripped the Douglass campus, and some of the faculty reverted to a defensive attitude which went all the way back to the days of Dean Douglass and had been a recurring phenomenon ever since. As late as 1959, Dean Bunting had found it necessary to point out in her Report to the President: "Probably the most acute source of poor morale at Douglass has been a sense that University decisions of vital importance to the college . . . have been made without consulting those best informed at the college." [3]

But slowly the acquired habit of mistrust gave way to a more realistic and hopeful assessment of the future. Dean Adams helped to promote the change by continually pointing out the advantages of membership in a university. At this writing, no final decision has been made by the University on the Federated Plan.

The Douglass Trustees' Committee meanwhile, with its alumnae members, was alert and diligent in safeguarding the College's interests. It continued the practice of inviting faculty and administration members not only to report on new educational ventures as in the past, but also to express their views on impending changes. It noted with approval the recommendation of the University auditors that Douglass retain its historic separate budget, since no savings would be effected by its elimination. And the Trustees' Committee echoed the sentiments of students and faculty in favoring a return to a separate Douglass commencement, after the experience of participating in the general University commencement in the Bicentennial year 1966.[4]

The President and Provost along with Dean Adams were meticulous about keeping the Douglass faculty informed of plans for the future of the University and of the College's share in these plans. All this had its effect. Most of the Douglass people came to see that to be one of a number of equal colleges, one that excelled in certain aspects of higher education, was an acceptable role which could be challenging and exciting. And so, when the establishment of Livingston, the first of the new colleges, was announced, the faculty adopted a resolution welcoming the newcomer and offering to share resources.[5]

For the individual faculty member the new era meant broader opportunities but also more rigorous demands. Douglass shared in the benefits of the University-wide building program. The new University library was open to its faculty and students. The even newer University Center for Computer and Information Services assisted a growing number of departments. But most important, the financial straitjacket of the Depression and the war years was finally thrown off; for though the College was far from rolling in luxury and though the legislature's appropriations continued to fall short of needs, some money was now available for study, research, and experimentation. The days of extreme penury, of hand-to-mouth existence, of making do by papering over the thin spots, of not venturing beyond the proved and the traditional for fear of courting financial disaster—those days were over. Reduced teaching schedules and leaves of absence, so rare in the earlier decades, were now achieved in department after department. With increasing frequency

Mrs. Edward J. Katzenbach with Dean Adams at Katzenbach Hall when the dormitory was dedicated in April 1963

Douglass professors and instructors sought and received grants for study and professional improvement. Nearest at hand was the Rutgers University Research Council with grants available to members of all the different faculties of the University. Others received aid from learned societies, the great private foundations, or the various instrumentalities of the Federal Government. The magic names of Ford, Fulbright, Guggenheim, National Science Foundation worked a transformation in the faculty of the College. Douglass professors could now be found working on research or teaching assignments in all parts of the United States, in England, Greece, India, Italy, Japan. Under these broadening experiences, year after year, the old narrow parochialism gradually broke down.

A similar purpose was served by a new administrative and policy-making device: the Section. This was a cross-sectional organization of professors in all colleges of the University grouped according to subject. Thus everybody teaching mathematics, whether at the colleges for men, at Douglass, Newark, Camden, or University College, was a member of the Mathematics Section. The chairman of the Section, elected by the membership, could be from any college, and Douglass professors headed several. The Federated College Plan of 1967 looked to the same end: the strengthening of New Brunswick-wide academic departments.

Though their programs and effectiveness varied considerably, the Sections conferred distinct benefits. For one, sectional pressure led to a gradual reduction of the sometimes excessive teaching loads at Douglass. It also became a gateway to graduate teaching. Ever since Dean Douglass and the Trustees' Committee had ordained, back in 1932, that Douglass undergraduates were entitled to the full time of their professors, those faculty members who aspired to share in the University graduate program had to do so on their own time, almost at their own risk. This situation gradually changed as the administration modified its rigid position and as the influence of the Sections grew.

Appointment to the faculty and promotion in rank had formerly rested solely upon recommendation by the department chairman and approval by the Dean; criteria for advancement were successful teaching and general usefulness to the College and the University. Now the emphasis was changing. The Section had to approve departmental recommendations before they came to the Dean, and the Section set up additional standards. It wanted to know whether the candidate had an active field of research and publication. Generally speaking, this was a legitimate requirement, for a principal function of any university is research in all fields of knowledge. Rutgers, The State University, had to have a faculty that was academically respectable and included a fair proportion of men and women with national reputations in their respective disciplines.

Yet the new emphasis created a dilemma for some. "Publish or perish," a cliché that oversimplified, nevertheless came to plague more than one conscientious teacher at Douglass. Publication presented difficulties, even when time for research and writing was forthcoming. It was less of a problem in the sciences. Here the results of an experiment, which to be sure might represent months of rigorous investigation by a competent specialist, could be written up in a few pages of one of the many scientific journals. But in the humanities the obstacles were more formidable. An essay in literary criticism or a historical article required many pages, and journals in these fields had backlogs running to years. University presses meanwhile, though not expected to show a profit, still had to operate within limited budgets and could not afford to publish every manuscript that came their way.

Then, too, the relationship between publishing and teaching was not always clear. This was particularly the case in the large freshman and sophomore courses in general education to which Douglass, as a liberal arts college, was committed. In these broadly inclusive courses, which introduced high school graduates to college methods and adult ways of thinking, good teaching was of critical importance, yet the necessarily narrow fields of research of most professors had little relevance. In advanced courses for upperclassmen one could plow the results of research back into one's lectures, even though the matter never got into print. Should the effectiveness of teachers who were alert to students' needs and also kept abreast of their disciplines be lost to the College for want of a sufficiently impressive list of their own publications? After all, no correlation had ever been established between the quantity of a professor's published research and his success as a teacher of undergraduates. The rosters of college faculty had always included professors who excelled as classroom teachers and others whose teaching was mediocre or worse; each category contained men and women with national reputations for their books as well as others who had scarcely published a line. Years ago, Alfred North Whitehead stated the case for the teacher who did not publish:

In every faculty you will find that some of the more brilliant teachers are not among those who publish. Their originality requires for its expression direct intercourse with their pupils in the form of lectures, or of personal discussion. Such men exercise an immense influence; and yet, after the generation of their pupils has passed away, they sleep among the innumerable unthanked benefactors of humanity. Fortunately, one of them is immortal—Socrates.[6]

The new dispensation raised other questions of educational policy. Douglass College had always insisted, almost as an article of faith, that its professors be accessible to their students and alert to campus issues. This was becoming more difficult. Involvement with graduate students left less time for the undergraduates; besides, graduate courses conferred prestige. The large generalized freshman and sophomore

courses, on the other hand, with their many sections, did
nothing to build up one's own field of research or professional reputation. Yet there always remained some who preferred undergraduate teaching as the true fulfillment of the
liberal arts philosophy. Accessibility to students was also a
function of residence. In the early years most of the faculty lived near the campus, in New Brunswick or Highland
Park. Now more and more came out from New York—especially the increasing number of part-time appointees—or
else they drove in from Princeton or other New Jersey subur-
ban communities, and were not so readily available for committee meetings, student conferences, and other chores
which had formerly been taken for granted.

Aware of these growing tendencies, administration and
faculty moved to counteract them where possible. With no
desire to return to an older defensive stance or to lose sight
of the broader professional vistas offered by the University,
they nevertheless continued to acknowledge their responsibility to their students. When in 1966 the *Alumnae Bulletin*
asked the five retiring faculty members of that year to
comment on their years at Douglass, all five, in one way
or another, reaffirmed the faculty's continuing concern for
their students. And it was not only the retirees who felt
this way; in the ranks of the younger members there
were many who took their obligations to the undergraduates
as seriously as the veterans. Dean Adams, in a Voorhees Assembly address recorded in the same issue of the *Bulletin*,
had this to say:

The faculty has a three-headed responsibility. As classroom
teachers they are to present with delight and relevance the material in the discipline to which they have chosen to devote
their lives. As scholars, faculty members have every right to say,

"Please go away because I am reading and I have to write. Please go away because I have to think.". . . As participators in community life the faculty members share committees with the students and take part in all-college programs. They turn up as auctioneers for fund raising projects, they meet with evaluating committees, they advise you both formally and informally. . . . They go beyond their instructional and scholarly commitments.[7]

On the lighter side, the faculty managed to let down their hair now and then, as in earlier days. A musical version of *Alice in Wonderland*, first done in 1953, with the title role played by a senior dramatic arts major, was repeated six years later, on the eve of Founders Day. The quadrennial Faculty Show for the benefit of the Campus Chest was revived in 1964.

By way of keeping channels of communication open, the faculty devised new machinery for guiding the freshmen. This had always been a vexatious issue and various methods of dealing with it had been tried over the years. Now two alternating academic counselors were appointed, each taking an entering class and carrying it through the sophomore year, at which point the chairmen of the students' major departments picked them up. Assisting the counselors was a committee of seventeen who, in small groups, met with corresponding freshman groups to give miscellaneous advice. Though too new to warrant any final judgment, this plan seemed to work better than anything tried heretofore.

The general curriculum saw some reorganization. While holding fast to the underlying principle of a broad grounding in the arts and sciences followed by a major concentration, the faculty introduced some refinements and flexibilities designed to provide more varied fare in the two underclass years and, in some fields, a later decision on the major subject. The traditional professional majors continued to attract their quota of students, and the various professional schools within the University were more fully exploited. None of this was very explosive; in basic matters the faculty remained conservative. The substance of the graduation requirements was left intact except insofar as individual departments changed the content of required courses. Proposals such as one to add geology to the group requirement in science, or another to make logic an alternative to mathematics, were turned down. Faculty conservatism was shown too in the defeat of a motion to substitute comprehensive departmental final examinations for the existing examinations in courses. The faculty also turned down a proposal to dismantle the College Council. After exhaustive discussion lasting through several meetings, what was salvaged from this proposal was the creation of a Long-Range Educational Planning Committee, very much like the old Educational Policies Committee of the nineteen-thirties, to take over that phase of the Council's work; the latter remained otherwise intact. Yet the faculty was not averse to all innovation. In 1966 it approved as a pilot project, with the aid of federal financing, the admission of twenty culturally deprived girls from low income families, who had not met the regular entrance requirements. These girls were given five years to complete the normal four-year course, under the guidance of a faculty director.[8]

Special programs for the highly gifted few, which the faculty had fostered from the earliest days, were endangered by rising enrollments and vocational pressures. They had always been hothouse plants, sensitive to the chilling blasts from the outside world of practical expediency. In an institution that catered to the middle and lower middle economic brackets, it was not easy to persuade even qualified students to embark on an esoteric venture that had so little cash value. The Freshman Seminar, so auspiciously begun, fell victim to this pressure. With it went its counterpart, the "Sour Grapes Seminar." The honors program languished, barely keeping pace with growing enrollments. A feature of the curriculum since the late nineteen-twenties, this program had enabled a few topflight seniors and an occasional junior to carry on individual investigations under tutorial guidance. Over the years it had turned out some excellent products. But, though offered by virtually every department in the College, it was not subsidized and had to be carried as an extra. Larger enrollments in the regular courses made it burdensome. To reanimate the honors work, Dean Adams, intensely interested in the honors program, had the former Physics Building remodeled into an Honors House, a retreat for honors candidates from all departments for undisturbed study, reflection, and exchange of ideas.

To understand what was going on in Douglass College in the nineteen-sixties a Cook's Tour of several departments of instruction might be helpful. The sciences continued to play an important role. Physics, to be sure, had been lost. Never a large department, it could not support the cost of the new electronic equipment for a handful of majors. After the death, in 1959, of Wilfred Jackson, the chairman, who had taught his subject not only for specialists but with a keen awareness of the needs of those who wanted physics as part of a liberal education, the Department was phased out. Douglass students interested in physics had to take their program at Rutgers.

As though to make up for the loss of physics, bacteriology

Honors House, one of the original buildings on the Carpender estate, was used for the Physics Department until the honors program was instituted by Dean Adams

became one of the fastest-growing departments; Hazel B. Gillespie was chairman. Jeff Swinebroad and his Department of Biological Sciences were unusually successful in articulating their offerings with those of the men's colleges. The introductory course in biology was given on both campuses by closed-circuit television. No one received as much in research grants as members of this department. In chemistry, Roger Sweet, ably seconded by Lillian N. Ellis, a valuable all-around member of the faculty, had long felt that the introductory course, part of the general education program, failed to give adequate preparation to chemistry majors. After long discussion the Chemistry Department had been given permission to step these courses up to a four-point potency. Bacteriology, biology, and botany followed suit in 1965–66. While all these departments were now in a better position to meet standards set by their several professional societies and thus to smooth the vocational path for their majors, this tilting of the balance, though slight, raised some questions about the underlying philosophy of a general education, since heretofore the obligatory courses for graduation in all academic subjects had been three-point courses. The whole matter was, of course, based on the assumption that one could measure the quality of an education by quantitative standards.

Mathematics continued as one of the larger departments, appealing annually to a considerable number of majors, who usually obtained good positions upon graduation.

The English Department, still the largest, continued to offer a wide range of courses in literature, criticism, and creative writing. In 1962 Elizabeth F. Boyd succeeded Donald C. Dorian as chairman. Miss Boyd had breadth of vision beyond the immediate needs of her department and was always in demand for difficult assignments and responsible posts. She was the first representative of the language and literature division on the College Council. Her community services included a twelve-week television lecture series on the modern novel. In addition to Miss Boyd there were Doris V. Falk, who taught Shakespeare, Nelle Smither, who taught modern drama, Anna Mary Wells, who taught creative writing, and twenty others, most of them recent arrivals.

Foreign languages expanded to include a full Department of Russian Language and Literature. Ludmilla B. Turkevich, its chairman, was supported by a staff of three. A Russian House and a Russian dining table took their places beside

A novel experiment in 1958 was a world poetry course prepared and taught by students

the French, the German, and the Spanish. Alumnae contributions helped put this department on its feet. French, Italian, and Spanish continued under the administrative umbrella of the Department of Romance Languages; chairman of the whole, from 1961, was Leonardo Santamarina, a Loyalist veteran of the Spanish Civil War.

The 'sixties saw a welcome renascence of the classical languages, which had been on the verge of disappearing from Douglass as well as from the colleges for men. Now, instruction in Latin and Greek for all branches of the University in New Brunswick was centered on the Douglass campus. Under the leadership of scholars like Smith Palmer Bovie, chairman, Anna S. Benjamin, and a group of younger members, a fresh set of course offerings appeared which not only rehabilitated the classics as such but undergirded history, literature, and philosophy and thus strengthened the humanistic flavor of a Douglass education.

History, still one of the large departments though now separated from political science, set its usual high standards. Its chairman, Thomas Weber, a veteran of the Afro-Italian campaign in the Second World War, taught Latin-American history; Margaret Hastings presided over the Middle Ages and kept alive her research in the English common law. New fields were opened with courses on China and on the Ottoman Empire. Meantime the freshman course continued to tax the resources and the imagination of the entire department. Four of the senior members taught and directed theses in the Graduate School.

Philosophy offered a more varied program. Courses in this department, headed now by Fadlou A. Shehadi, displayed both familiarity with new analytical trends and a continued awareness of the humanistic origins of the discipline.

There was ferment in the social sciences. For several years an experimental course crossing departmental lines was offered to a select group of students; analytical in nature, it attempted to find the common denominator of economics, political science, and sociology. It succumbed to the usual malaise of interdepartmental courses: mechanical problems of class scheduling, the difficulty of fusing the subject matter, and the preoccupation of the instructors with their own disciplines.

The Economics-Sociology Department continued to expand and diversify under the chairmanship of Richard M. Stephenson, who took office after Francis W. Hopkins retired and Harry C. Bredemeier began to devote most of his time to the University's Urban Studies Center. Next to English, sociology majors were the most numerous. Psychology, where Nelson G. Hanawalt and, upon his retirement in 1966, Edith D. Neimark led an alert staff, moved in the direction of experimental and other quantitative methods.

Political science courses stressed political behavior and subordinated mere description of political institutions and practices. The subject had always been a lively one at Douglass since the New Deal days, when some of the courses were conducted with evangelical fervor. It was in those days that a senior once urged a sophomore to take the International Relations course because then she would be able to worry about everything that was wrong all over the world. In the new dispensation the concern was still there, but it was disciplined by rigorous insistence on scientific analysis. The first chairman of the Department, Neil A. McDonald, came from Harvard, where he had coedited a volume of documents in political theory; before that he had been the youngest member of the last bicameral legislature in his native Nebraska, and later Public Works Administrator for the state. A scholar of balanced judgment and keen professional conscience, McDonald soon became one of the "anchor men" of the faculty, both in College and University. Closely associated with him was James N. Rosenau, who combined a genuine interest in his students—he married one—with thorough familiarity with the latest computerized techniques and was prolific in research and publication.

The Douglass Department of Speech and Dramatic Art had become University wide in its scope, and as the University Department of Drama conducted the traditional public performances of plays ancient, recent, and experimental in the Little Theater. Productions there ranged from Sophocles, Shakespeare, and Sheridan to Ibsen, Shaw, and Thurber. The Department's offerings expanded to include radio

Students majoring in Speech Therapy, one of the important innovations of the 'sixties, practice on the audiometer

and television broadcasting. Speech thereapy became an important major program under the direction of an alumna, Dorothy Taylor Durand '40, now chairman of the Department. Mrs. Durand also conducted a well-equipped Speech and Hearing Center for which she had received large grants, and where majors obtained clinical experience by working with speech-handicapped children and adults both at the Center and at various off-campus points.

Music flourished under the direction of Arnold Kunrad Kvam. The Department's enlarged program of historical, theoretical, and practical music was sufficiently professional to earn memership in the National Association of Schools of Music, yet left room for enough general college work to permit its majors to graduate with a liberal arts degree. Audio aids were modernized by the use of tapes, which were more flexible than the old-style records. The departmental library included a rare collection of vocal music and was building toward complete editions of the major composers. The faculty cooperated with the other arts: one of its members wrote the music for several Little Theater productions. The chairman conducted the Chapel Choir, as always, and the public recitals and community services of its members continued to provide cultural stimulus.

In a like manner the Art Department carried on its twofold function. To a widely ranging program of art history and theory it added a full complement of studio courses in drawing, painting, sculpture, graphics, and ceramics. These

Douglass women sing in University Choir, shown here with the Philadelphia Orchestra conducted by Eugene Ormandy

practical courses, like the corresponding ones in music, served all the units of the University in New Brunswick. Forty graduate students were enrolled in 1966. The faculty, made up of practicing artists, was led by Reginald H. Neal, chairman and University Professor of Art, and Robert G. Bradshaw, senior member in length of service.

No field of instruction, with the exception of Greek and Latin, was growing faster than that of religion, a post-World-War-II addition to the roster of departments. By 1967 it consisted of a chairman, Cyrus R. Pangborn, a lecturer, and four instructors. With courses that examined the history and philosophy of religion as well as its relation to science and to the culture of the day, the Department justified itself as a valid component of a liberal education. It also took the lead in effecting changes in the Voorhees Chapel assembly program. When Dean Bunting took office, she elected to preside over the so-called secular assembly on Thursdays only and delegated the Tuesday religious service to the chairman of the Department of Religion. This was a break with tradition. Dean Douglass had, in the manner of college presidents from time immemorial, conducted chapel as a matter of course, for she considered it a means of keeping communications open, building morale, and creating a sense of community. Dean Corwin, with some misgiving, had followed the example of her predecessor. But now a Voorhees Assembly Board of students and faculty was set up to supply this service. Under the leadership of the chairman of the Department of Religion, the Board selected an annual theme and built a program around it. Religious in the broadest sense of the word, even though the outward trappings—procession, hymns, prayers—were abandoned as regular practice, these programs dealt with contemporary trends in theology, comparative religions, personal ethics, and contemporary social issues.

But over the years, "chapel" programs became "assembly" programs and specialists and other knowledgeable speakers took up such widely ranging topics as civil rights and racism, changing attitudes toward sex, the nature of the mystical experience. The last-named included one meeting on the ultramodern phenomenon of psychedelic séances. By examining, without fear or favor, controversial questions of real concern to the students, be they novelties that commanded widespread support or traditional practices that stirred deep resentment, the assembly program became the conscience of the college. It swept nothing under the rug; but neither did it support the kind of half-informed emotional social protest that exhausted itself in highly publicized parades and placard-waving self-dramatization. As befitted an academic

"Date with Dad," popular spring event of the 'fifties and 'sixties

community, the Douglass assembly program said in effect: come let us reason together and try to discover for our day the old classical trinity of the beautiful, the good, and the true.

A new experience for the faculty was an increasing number of students from the colleges for men. In 1966, 825 students from other divisions of the University enrolled in courses at the women's college, while 564 Douglass students took one or more courses each "across town." The numbers varied from department to department. Those that had no representation on the Douglass campus at all naturally drew the most. Thus sixty-two women studied in the School of Journalism, fifty-one took Hebrew and 116 took physics at the College of Arts and Sciences; conversely, 201 Rutgers students sat in Greek and Latin classes, 174 in courses in religion, and twenty-five in dramatic arts: all of them subjects that were to be had only at Douglass. Some departments achieved an almost even exchange; in history, for example, fifty-eight Rutgers students took some of their courses at Douglass, while fifty-two Douglassites traveled across town. The corresponding figures for political science were thirty-one and twenty-six. There was some exchange, too, in English, mathematics, and biology. Modern languages, on the other hand, showed scarcely any cross-registration, for here the Douglass practice of conducting every class entirely in the foreign language was a barrier.

By and large, the "new" faculty of the nineteen-sixties was competent, scholarly, and interesting. It was better equipped than its predecessors who, were they to return to campus, would have marveled at the well-lighted and ventilated new class and lecture rooms, the microfilm viewers in the library, the televised lectures in the sciences, the up-to-date audio aids in the Music Building, the splendidly equipped Speech and Hearing Center, the computer-expedited work in the social sciences, and the Language Laboratory. The latter, set up in Arts Building in quarters vacated by the library, was exceptionally good. Having delayed the introduction of phonic devices and recording machinery longer than some colleges, the language departments were able to avoid the mistakes and inadequacies of pioneer equipment and installed a well-tested system when they finally moved into this field.

The faculty, old and new, was not a collection of recluses or unworldly denizens of ivory towers. For all the pressures of their profession, many kept one foot outside the campus and pursued civic interests or pleasant avocations. A sampling will have to suffice. Of the older faculty, Frank Hopkins had done tax studies for the State of New Jersey; George Schmidt had conducted summer seminars for foreign students under the auspices of the American Friends Service Committee. Currently, Emery Battis, director of the American Studies program, who had come to academic life from the theater, was playing leads in summer Shakespeare festivals and repertory in Princeton during the winter. Marina Romero, professor of Spanish, was a poet of stature with seven volumes of verse to her credit. Anna Mary Wells of the English Department not only taught creative writing but practiced it as the author of a scholarly literary biography and many volumes of highly regarded mystery fiction. Neil McDonald and Thomas Weber entered politics in their home communities; the former was president of the Edison Township Council, the latter mayor of Metuchen.

Student life in the nineteen-sixties, like everything else about the College, was affected by the tremendous increase

Members of the first four graduating classes at the fortieth reunion of the Class of 1922. At far right is Alice J. Aronoff, Assistant Dean Emeritus

in numbers. This created problems that taxed the resources and the ingenuity of administration and student leaders alike. Practices and institutions designed for a campus of one thousand needed to be retested and modified to meet the needs of one almost three times as large.

Academic standards, already high, were rising, for the College continued to draw the great majority of its students from the upper tenth of New Jersey high schools, and the high schools were getting better. When the Soviet Union launched the first earth satellite in October of 1957, it shocked American educators into a breast-beating reexamination of the work of their hands, which in turn produced a widespread reorganization of content and method, especially in mathematics and the sciences. This meant, in time, better prepared high school graduates and a higher quality of college freshmen.

Student intellectual interests and awareness of academic responsibility manifested themselves in a variety of ways. A novel experiment, in 1958, was a world poetry course, conceived, organized, offered, and elected by students. Ten upperclassmen taught the course, including several foreign students who presented recent poetry of their native lands. Due recognition came to this experiment when it was awarded first prize by the National Student Association as a prime example of undergraduate intellectual activity. Also on the extracurricular front, a new journal was launched: *Promethean.* An outlet for the social sciences, the new publication took its place beside *Horn Book*, which was usually monopolized by English majors. In 1962 a series of independent reading groups was organized, of five to ten each; with commendable catholicity of taste the first group started in on Dante and J. D. Salinger.[9]

Commencement on Antilles Field, June 1963

Apart from organized groups, general reading habits improved, spurred by the proliferation of paperback books which put the literary classics as well as recent works within easy reach at the Student Co-operative Book Store. Paperbacks also facilitated expanding assignments in English, history, and other subjects. An extreme instance of the new intellectual pride occurred in 1962, when the campus newspaper took issue with the alumnae for their alleged lack of interest in things of the mind. The *Alumnae Bulletin* had published an article reporting mother-and-daughter reactions to the general theme of campus customs then and now, and *Caellian* was sharply critical. In none too temperate language the editor berated the alumnae—most unfairly, the latter thought—for a soggy sentimentality which concerned itself only with tradition while ignoring the intellectual core of campus life.[10]

For years the students had attempted, through Government Association committees or otherwise, to convey to the faculty such desires as arose among them for change and innovation in the curriculum. Attempts to evaluate individual professors and courses had also occurred as far back as the nineteen-thirties. None of these devices had been consistently applied. Moments of sporadic zeal by an energetic committee chairman were followed by periods of inactivity. In the mid-nineteen-sixties an active student curriculum committee brought some of these issues back to life. Bolstered by facts and arguments which this committee had assembled, Government Association asked for a number of changes, including a more varied freshman program, the elimination of fines for missing classes before and after holidays, and of final examinations for seniors in the second semester. They also asked that students be allowed to take some electives without being expected to achieve more than a passing grade. The general philosophy of a liberal education, they argued, warranted all this.

The students' suggestions met with a favorable response. The faculty took them seriously and adopted most, in whole or in part. Holiday fines were abolished, and class attendance was left to the discretion of the individual instructor. To some professors this marked an advance toward maturity, but others deplored it as an unfortunate lowering of standards and a complete abdication of faculty responsibility. The freshman program was diversified; upperclassmen were permitted to take one course each term on a pass-fail basis; and a poll showed two-thirds of the faculty giving at least qualified support to student evaluation of professors and courses.

But the request to excuse seniors from final examinations was denied as "academically unsound." [11]

Campus life went on as before within the framework of Government Association, that overall structure of administration, faculty, and student body, each with its separate obligations and degree of authority. But active participation by the faculty was slackening. At the annual election in 1965, 1,327 students, fifteen administration and five faculty members voted for president of Government Association. Yet the motion by a faculty representative that the Assembly eliminate faculty and administration membership and become exclusively a student organization was defeated.[12]

Like American undergraduates of this decade generally, Douglass students were seeking identity, and some felt alienation. *Caellian* called the tune, reminding its readers at the beginning of a school year that all college activity had one common purpose: the "discovery of who we are." [13] In the opinion of some of the more perceptive younger faculty members who had previously taught in other eastern colleges, their Douglass students were highly intelligent, industrious, and concerned. They had the courage to question inherited values and beliefs, but expected to distill from their courses better and more permanent values for themselves and for society, just as their parents expected their college education to place them on a more secure economic footing. They were less interested in pursuing an argument in a philosophy or a literature or a history course to all its possible conclusions, merely as an exercise in mental calisthenics or for the sheer pleasure of the pursuit. Wholly disinterested intellectual fencing comes more easily to students cushioned by several generations of economic security; Douglass girls were willing to ask questions, but they wanted Answers.

In fairness to them one might ask how many professors at Douglass, or at any other college, were able and willing to encourage and sustain such adventures of the mind.

The Honor System was again under fire, as so many times before in its forty-year reign. In an attempt to meet the challenge of new circumstances it had to carry a heavier load of responsibility and began to creak under the strain. The success of the system had always depended on an overwhelming consensus which in turn rested upon a sense of community and separateness. All this was weakening for a variety of reasons. There was the student body, more than doubled in size, nearly half of whom lived in new, comparatively luxurious dormitories and ate in their own dining hall instead of meeting all their fellows three times a day at table in Cooper Hall. Commuters, not subject to the social regulations of dormitory life, were more numerous than ever. Meanwhile, hundreds of girls enrolled in courses at Rutgers, which had no honor system, and hundreds of Rut-

Aerial view of the present Douglass College

gers students were finding their way into Douglass classes. Isolation was breaking down, and that select and somewhat remote community which Douglass College had been was succumbing to the world's slow stain.

Under these cumulative pressures a major reexamination of the Honor System got under way in 1962, and the issue was joined, once again, over the reporting clause. The obligation to report oneself or others when an offense was committed had never been popular, but had been accepted as the only means of securing collective responsibility. Dean Bunting had had her doubts about it, calling it an obligatory community police system whose aims were worthy but whose machinery was often naïve. Dean of Students Marjorie Trayes, on the other hand, expressed serious doubts about the viability of any honor system without the reporting clause; to her this was the heart of the convenant.[14]

Now there was widespread suspicion that it was not working. The editor of *Caellian* proclaimed the system outworn: "The reporting clause is dead. Let's bury it." and again: "The prescriptions of the academic honor system are . . . insipid." [15] The faculty, alarmed, addressed itself to the problem. Concerned primarily with the academic features of the system as a safeguard of honesty in laboratory, library, and class examinations, the faculty reaffirmed its commitment to the principle in a resolution which included the following statement on the reporting clause:

Any member of the college community who observes or knows of an infraction of the academic regulations or principles of the honor system is responsible for asking the person involved to report the situation, or is responsible for notifying the student involved of her intention to report the situation.[16]

Though this remained the official faculty position, some members, especially recent appointees, were lukewarm in such numbers that Dean Adams felt compelled to comment. "Honor Board," she said, "again earned the respect of the college community for the thoroughness and good sense with which it handled its cases. One difficulty with the Honor System intensifies as the college grows: faculty, particularly new faculty, do not take the system or their responsibilities under it seriously . . ." [17]

In the following year, *Caellian* conducted a comprehensive poll which listed all the academic and social offenses mentioned in the *Red Book*, asked each student how frequently she had committed any of these or had seen them committed, and whether she had reported the offense or intended to report such offenses in the future. The disclosures were enlightening. In the area of social regulations the reporting clause was virtually inoperative. It succeeded better in curbing academic offenses but even there left something to be desired. Two out of three promised in future to report anyone cheating in tests, but less than one in four to report such infractions as smoking in unauthorized places, nonobservance of study hours, taking an apple out of the dining room, or failing to sign out when leaving the dormitory in the evening. Yet cheating was universally condemned, and only about 5 per cent admitted, even anonymously, that they had ever cheated or plagiarized.[18]

Government Association now took up the matter. After a long debate, the Assembly disassociated itself from the extreme views of the editor of *Caellian* and reaffirmed belief in the basic principle: "Resolved that the 1962–1963 Government Association Assembly affirm its positive support of the honor philosophy at Douglass." The essence of this philosophy, the resolution went on to say, was personal integrity and responsibility. At the same time the Assembly recognized the unwillingness of most students to accept all the responsibilities inherent in the system. It therefore recommended renewed orientation of the entire College community in the meaning and value of the honor concept, and suggested such modifications as were necessary to make the system realistic and workable. A few weeks later the newly elected Assembly for 1963–1964 voted its full support of this position.[19]

The chief difficulty, in the opinion of many—faculty as well as students—lay in the tendency to make the honor code support too many petty regulations which had no ethical content. With increasing enrollments the number of such regulations also increased, but they were always subject to change and opinions differed widely as to their value. To be successful, the Honor System must not be made to carry more than the traffic would bear. It should be confined to those standards of conduct, in class and in living quarters, on which there was general consensus. So far as possible, the twilight zone between ethical principle and administrative regulation should be eliminated.

A new and unforeseen test of the Honor System grew out of a change in campus eating habits. In 1961 the purchasing of food and the preparing and serving of meals in Cooper and Neilson dining halls were taken over by a University-wide bureaucratic organization: University Food Services. This meant more than a mere change of cooks, for Cooper was more than a dining hall: it was an institution, a ritual. Here, for thirty years, the students gathered from all the campuses three times a day, to sit at tables served by student waitresses, to hear news and exchange gossip. The food

was prepared by a devoted staff. The steward, Joseph Lasagna, was a culinary artist who bought only the best of
ingredients, spurned steam tables, and somehow took the
curse off mass-produced food and gave it a touch of home
cooking; in more recent years, Mr. Frank Caselli, manager of
Cooper, accomplished the same miracle. The waitresses were
carefully chosen and waitress captains were often student
leaders; as liaison between the eating multitudes and the
kitchen staff they played an important role. All this was
changed when University Food Services took over. Break-
fast and lunch were now served cafeteria style to provide
smoother adjustment with class schedules; waitresses checked
in on a clock, all in the name of efficiency and economy.
The impersonality of the new regulations, their brusqueness
and inflexibility, made staff and waitresses unhappy. And
the meals, said the critics, were poorer. The waitresses grew
so indignant at being reduced from valued participants to
underlings and robots that they took the unprecedented step
of threatening a strike. The vote was 81 to 12. At this, Food
Services withdrew the most objectionable rules, and the strike
was called off.[20]

The Honor System became involved when Food Services
began to issue meal tickets, checked students into the dining
halls, and claimed the right to see their identification cards.
Most obnoxious, students were prohibited from taking out
food to their roommates, a practice as old as the College
itself. Why, students asked, was one not allowed to eat the
food one had paid for, whether in the dining room or in the
dormitory? Manipulation of tickets and cards to facilitate
this did not seem a heinous offense. Yet Government Association decided, after extended debate, that it was dis-
honest, and the definition of lying, in the *Red Book*, was

enlarged to include "illegal use of Douglass identification card, misuse of meal ticket." [21] But many disagreed.

By way of offsetting this increase in bureaucratic controls, regulations in another area were simplified. Overnight absences from campus had hitherto involved a formidable complex of requests, permissions, and signatures, all growing out of the *in loco parentis* principle. All this machinery was now dismantled and a general statement of permission, understood and agreed to by students, parents, and College administration, was held to be sufficient. Unadministered overnight permission, so the Dean announced in April of 1966, was now a policy of the College.[22]

A few years before this liberalization an attempt had been made to reduce the restraints surrounding another kind of activity, but that one failed. Smoking, at one time a major offense as serious as lying or cheating, had become respectable in 1930, and permission to smoke had since then been extended to more and more buildings and areas. Now students wanted to include the living rooms of those dormitories that were fire-resistant. This meant Jameson and the four residence halls of Neilson Campus. A resolution to this effect, after an affirmative vote by the Assembly, a caveat by the Board of Review, and a second endorsement by the Assembly, finally reached Dean Adams' desk, and she vetoed it. A storm broke. *Caellian* announced, in a screaming headline reminiscent of the belligerent years of *Campus News:* "Adams Vetoes Smoking." An accompanying editorial refused to accept the Dean's reasons and concluded that "student government has in effect been abolished." Searching questions were raised in Assembly as to the purpose and scope of Government Association. A flood of letters in successive issues of *Caellian* denounced the

Dean's ruling. One of the more desperate ones maintained: "The United States is changing. The Catholic Church is changing. The Soviet Union is changing. Africa is changing. Asia is changing. Even the shoreline of New Jersey is changing! Douglass, steeped in its tradition, is stagnating." And amid the torrent of denunciation one lone letter of gratitude to the Dean, from two nonsmokers.

To meet the criticism, Dean Adams announced an open meeting. Though widely publicized, the meeting attracted only 250 students, less than 10 per cent of the whole. Thirty faculty members also came. Here the Dean explained and defended her veto. The rights of nonsmokers must be protected, smokers had enough places on campus. The fire hazard remained, for fire-resistant did not mean fireproof. Finally, in the light of growing medical evidence that cigarettes were a health menace, it would be unwise to reduce the curbs on the practice still further. Inasmuch as the Dean smoked cigarettes herself, no one could question her impartiality. She went on to explain the role of student government in the context of the whole University and suggested a committee to review the relationship. Such a committee was created, but found little response from students, and the burning issue died down.[23]

Campus life was not all meetings and resolutions on smoking and overnight leaves. There was a lively social calendar and it reflected the temper of the times. Students from Rutgers and other nearby colleges found their way to the "Coop" for dates and dances as they always had. Like their contemporaries everywhere, they did the twist, the frug, the watusi, and other primitive contortions, to the tuneless rhythms of rock and roll. The traditional Christmas formal was now a single event, in Neilson Dining Hall and later in the enlarged College Center. When the folk-music revival, with its steel guitars and mop-headed performers, swept the country, Douglass had its share of devotees. Competitive athletics, though it existed in a limited way, was not a major interest. Students went to Rutgers football and basketball games in considerable numbers, as they always had, and the proposal for girl cheerleaders caused an occasional stir, only to die down again. The stance of the sophisticated Douglass-ite was one of aloof tolerance, though she might not go as far as the editorial writer in *Caellian* who dismissed the annual Princeton game with one sentence: "The fifty-seventh football game between Rutgers and Princeton will ruin the grass again this year on the Palmer Stadium field, and several thousand students will jubilantly celebrate each play, whatever its outcome." [24]

Much of the enthusiasm that athletics failed to generate went into public affairs and social reforms. This could hardly have been otherwise in view of the College's location. Douglass was no ivory tower, no Shangri-la. Members of a university situated in the heart of the megalopolis of the Eastern seaboard, with the *New York Times* a daily companion, Douglass students had the world's problems at their doorstep. Experts and authorities from universities, government, and industry came to the campus to lecture and lead discussions, sponsored by departmental clubs, by the International Weekend Committee, by the Voorhees Assembly Board. True, the student lecture series dating back to the nineteen-thirties had been given up and its appropriation diverted by Government Association to a general University lecture fund; this practice in turn had been discontinued when the students decided they did not like the type of lecturer brought to Rutgers. But in a large measure the Tuesday and Thursday assembly programs and the International Week End made up for this loss. In addition, Douglass held membership in the middle-of-the-road National Student Association; the organization of the "new left," Students for a Democratic Society, had no chapter on campus, though students could join the Rutgers chapter.

For more than a decade following the Second World War, discussion of public affairs was muffled and the normal undergraduate zeal for controversial issues subsided. Chief reason, as mentioned in an earlier chapter, was the wave of reaction associated with the name of the late Senator Joseph McCarthy of Wisconsin which for a time made the espousal of unpopular ideas hazardous. By about 1960 this wave had spent itself, for the time being, and student opinion all over the United States was once more asserting itself with vigor and enthusiasm, spilling over in a few cases into an unreasonable opposite extreme. Douglass students by and large were not extremists, but they were increasingly concerned.

The two principal issues that roused student interest in the 'sixties were civil rights and war in Vietnam. Not that there was much controversy over the first: the College solidly supported constitutional rights for Negroes as well as the legislative measures designed to secure them. Vietnam provoked wider differences of opinion. On the race issue, the student newspaper ran front-page stories of southern marches and riots; mass meetings were held in Voorhees Chapel; Government Association passed resolutions; Negro leaders spoke on campus; and faculty participated in panel discussions. A few students and professors picketed and joined protest marches, but by and large the Douglass student was not the placard-carrying type. College facilities were occasionally made available to off-campus organizations. Thus Hickman Hall became the scene of a panel debate conducted by the American Civil Liberties Union and open to the public. The moderator was a Princeton professor, participants included a controversial Rutgers professor, a Communist Party leader, a one-time Republican candidate for governor of New Jersey, and the Conservative Party's candidate for the United States Senate.[25]

Controversy flamed high when the "teach-in" reached Rutgers University in 1965. An impromptu medium for giving expression to hitherto latent student and faculty opposition to the war in Vietnam, the teach-in spread like a brush fire over American campuses. Open meetings, beginning late in the evening, would last through the night, or as long as any one was left to talk or listen. At the first of these on the Rutgers campus, a professor of history who described himself as a Marxist and a Socialist, expressed the hope that the National Liberation Front would win control of South Vietnam. His views provoked a storm of criticism throughout the State. The Republican candidate for governor—it was an election year—made the incident a campaign issue and demanded that the University discharge the "seditious" professor. The incumbent Governor left the decision to the University authorities, and the latter, resisting public clamor, maintained the principle of academic freedom and refused to discharge the professor, even though they disagreed with his opinions and tactics.

Student and faculty opinion at Douglass supported this stand, by a vote of 775–41 and 65–1 respectively as an N.S.A. poll disclosed. *Caellian* took the same view, without growing hysterical. In a sane editorial it questioned whether "a long chain of teach-ins alone can serve the cause of free speech." Students, the editor went on, instead of defying the reactionary public, should try to explain academic freedom to the citizens of New Jersey. "We should reassure the public that Rutgers is not the hotbed of Communism some political figures have described. A minority of students heard Genovese's and Mellen's [26] controversial remarks; a much smaller minority agreed . . . and there were no converts to Marxism." The editor seemed to have interpreted campus opinion fairly well; at any rate a statement in support of the Administration's Vietnam policy drew seven hundred Douglass signatures. Later teach-ins attempted to redress the balance with scholarly presentations of all aspects of the issue by specialists from within and without the University. Douglass professors participated in these and similar attempts to preserve academic detachment: James N. Rosenau of the Political Science Department spoke on problems of American foreign policy, and Jessie Lutz, a specialist in Chinese history, lectured on "The East Wind, the West Wind, and China." [27]

State issues received some attention, especially those concerned with financial support of the University. *Caellian* editorialized, and the Government Association Assembly passed resolutions, on bond referenda and broad-based taxes. But neither took a partisan stand in national elections; groups labeled Young Democrats and Young Republicans stirred some passing interest in election years. [28]

On the whole, the students of Douglass remained level-headed in trying times and conducted their lives, as Dean Adams once put it, "with sense and dignity," even though they were acutely aware of the Damocles Sword of the Bomb and questioned the wisdom of their elders who had allowed the world to come to such a pass. No doubt there were among them, as in nearly any group of nearly three

thousand young people, the usual delayed adolescents, con-
genital rebels, bleeding hearts, and irrepressible exhibition-
ists. But these were a minority. An occasional shrill voice
was raised in *Caellian*, but as a rule the student paper talked
sense. The beatnik era came and went, always a fringe activity. Open meetings and forums went off the rails now
and then, when feelings ran high. When, for an instance,
the proposed plan of "federated colleges" was first disclosed
to the students, in February of 1967, it roused considerable
opposition. While much of this was uninformed, some grew
out of the fear that classes at Douglass might increasingly fall
into the hands of inexperienced instructors and graduate
assistants.[29] But sooner or later, burning issues such as this
had a way of reaching the level of rational discussion, and
grievances and proposals for change were aired in orderly
fashion.

Some students satisfied their social conscience with action
rather than talk. At the opening of the school year in 1964,
for example, two hundred volunteered for community service of one kind or another in New Brunswick. But strikes,
picketing, and "nonviolent" disorderliness were rare. There
were those, too, who plodded through their college years
impervious to the roaring world about them. They went to
no meetings, voted in no elections, avoided all controversy; their one concern was to pass their courses and get
a job or a husband when they graduated.

Service to College and community continued to character-
ize the alumnae, who were growing in numbers and influence. By 1967 they totaled 11,500. Their organization, the
Associate Alumnae, worked in close harmony with the College authorities, and its Executive Director and the Editor
of the *Alumnae Bulletin* were authorized to attend all fac-

ulty meetings. In the manner of college alumni everywhere, the association made regular financial contributions. These were not large at first, for the organization was very young when hit by the Depression; besides, it shared the difficulties of alumnae of all women's colleges in that the married graduates did not as a rule control the family finances, and priorities had a way of going to the husband's alma mater. In the face of such handicaps, the contributions were noteworthy. They included the annual alumnae scholarships as well as the fund for the professional and cultural enrichment of the faculty mentioned in an earlier chapter. Of increasing importance was the unrestricted Dean's Fund as annual reunion class gifts poured into it; from this fund glaring needs could be met that were left unfulfilled by the all-too-tight State appropriations, and it also made possible educational programs and experiments of various kinds. In 1966–67 the first Visiting Associate Alumnae Lecturer, Dr. Tsune Shirai, psychologist from Tokyo Women's Christian College, was brought to the campus by the Dean's Fund.

The Associate Alumnae cooperated in Alumnae College, a Douglass program of lectures and discussions by members of the faculty on the two days preceding Reunion Day in June, all by way of refreshing alumnae interest in contemporary problems and things of the mind. The association maintained contact with its membership by means of an elaborate committee system and a large Board of Directors. The high rate of participation thus achieved was reflected in the numbers that contributed. In the early 1960's this was running about 50 per cent, almost twice the rate of participation by alumni of state universities generally. In recognition of this achievement the Associate Alumnae was awarded first prize by the American Alumni Council for "distinguished achievement in the development of alumni support." [30] Other awards included a first place in the category of sustained performance among public institutions; this came in 1966. The *Alumnae Bulletin* meanwhile, begun as a four-page mimeographed issue in February of 1926, had grown into a highly presentable alumnae magazine. Under a succession of competent editors it too achieved a variety of prizes and awards.

Although its president no longer served automatically on the University's Board of Trustees, the New Jersey State Federation of Women's Clubs continued its active interest in the College. The Federation's administrative organization still included the Douglass College Committee, and the general membership contributed funds to the building of the Student Center, to furnishings of the new Library, and to scholarships. The Pan American Scholarship and others in music, art, and various subjects, all of long standing, were augmented by a general scholarship fund under auspices of the College Committee. And College Day in the fall, when Federation members brought prospective students to the campus from all parts of the State, remained a feature of the College calendar.

The Douglass administration was at pains to maintain contact with those groups in the State most interested in the higher education of women. Dean Bunting had initiated meetings with representatives of these groups, and Dean Adams continued to meet at least once a year with representatives of each of the following: the Federation of Women's Clubs, the Business and Professional Women, the Federation of Colored Women's Clubs, the League of Women Voters, the Council of Jewish Women, the Association of American University Women, the Congress of Parents and Teachers, the Young Women's Christian Association, the New Jersey Education Association, and the Federated District Boards of Education. It was all in the tradition set by Dean Douglass in the earliest days. Thus, channels were kept open and the College was able to explain to all interested parties what it was trying to do: offer a liberal education as well as preprofessional training of high caliber to as many qualified young women of New Jersey as could be accommodated.

In March of 1966, Dean Adams announced to a specially called faculty meeting that she was resigning her office as of July 1 to become President of Wellesley College. In an accompanying valedictory she summed up her impression of the institution she was leaving: "Douglass is a superior college, part of a university that is potentially great." She had helped make it so. Her goal from beginning to end was a college in which the arts and sciences were taught in lively fashion by competent scholars. Whenever occasion offered, she exhorted her colleagues to concentrate on the relevance and significance of their teaching to human life. She expected the faculty to take the initiative in educational policy, encouraged especially the younger members to speak their minds, and was keenly disappointed if the expected leadership failed to materialize. At the same time she was a clear-sighted administrator with a broad grasp of issues; her annual reports were analytical, forthright, and written with style. In them she deplored "the pall of authority" that kept younger faculty members from speaking up in meeting, characterized various departments as "serene," or "marking time," or "a perfect headache," or "the best in the college;" an administrative coworker was "a universal genius," a department chairman "petrifyingly dull." She steered Douglass into the mainstream of University involvement, but saw to it that the Dean remained captain of the ship.

In casting about for someone to carry on during the impending interregnum—the machinery for selecting a new Dean of the College moved slowly—the University made a happy choice. Professor Margaret A. Judson had retired that June—or thought she had—and was about to move on to a visiting professorship at the University of Michigan when President Gross invited her to stay on as Acting Dean. She accepted and threw herself into the new work with customary vigor. Hers was not a caretaker administration, and this was fortunate. In the College Council and in faculty meeting she worked to make the faculty, particularly its many new members, more concerned with the College as a whole. In the Provost's Planning Committee, where the reorganization of the New Brunswick colleges was being hammered out, Dean Judson's long experience and thorough grasp of the problem stood the College in good stead. In appreciation of the "great service" which she had rendered during this year of transition, the faculty raised a substantial sum to establish in her name an annual prize in history.

The new Dean of the College as of the opening of the 1967–68 year was Margery Somers Foster, a native of Boston and a graduate of Wellesley with a Ph.D. in economics from Radcliffe. In the course of her professional career, which included both teaching and administration, she held office at various times at Mount Holyoke, Harvard, and Wellesley, and came to Douglass from her most recent post, that of Dean of Hollins College. An active participant in several

Margaret A. Judson, Emeritus Professor of History and
Acting Dean of the College, 1966–1967

263

Margery Somers Foster, Dean of the College, 1967–

groups investigating various aspects of current American higher education, she had made a special study of the role of women's colleges.

And so, as its fifth Dean took the helm, Douglass College entered its fiftieth year.

～～ Notes

CHAPTER I

1. Frank N. Bowles, "New Jersey's Educational Climate Must Change," *Douglass Alumnae Bulletin*, Summer 1958.
2. Much of this story is in the *Personal Recollections* of Mrs. Douglass, first printed in the N.J.C. yearbook, *Quair*, for 1929.
3. Minutes of the Jersey City College Club, May 17, 1912.
4. Archie Rice, *Home News*, Nov. 8, 1912.
5. Mrs. Clausine M. Macneille to President Demarest, Dec. 7, 1914.
6. Letters to Fred R. Cutchem, Jan. 10, 1914, and to E. B. Coe, Feb. 27, 1914.
7. Frelinghuysen to Demarest, March 26, 1914.
8. Minutes, Jersey City College Club, Oct. 25, 1912; Douglass letter to Demarest, July 24, 1913.
9. Trustees' resolution, Jan. 12, 1915.
10. Letter from Mrs. C. W. Stockton recorded in trustees' minutes, June 15, 1915.
11. Douglass letters to Demarest, Nov. 19, and Dec. 22, 1914, July 24, 1913.
12. Robert Scoon, *The Need of a College for Women* (23 pp. pamphlet), 1917.
13. Letters of Mrs. Marvin to Demarest, June 7, Oct. 8, 1915; to Mrs. Ada English, librarian of Douglass College, April 21, 1943.
14. Elmer Boyd to Demarest, Aug. 5, 1915.

15. Douglass, *Personal Recollections* (see note 2), p.13.
16. Trustees' minutes, April 12, 1918; Frelinghuysen to Demarest, Feb. 16, 1918.
17. Demarest to Dean Gildersleeve, May 4, 1918.
18. Trustees' minutes, April 12, 1918; Mrs. English interview with Demarest.
19. Alfred P. Skinner to Demarest, April 15, 1918.
20. The nickname, according to various alumnae who suffered it gladly, was either derived from Cooper Hall, where some students were housed for a while, or from the idea of a women's college as a hen coop.
21. Letter of Acting President of Rutgers Philip Brett to Miss Margaret Buttenheim, June 9, 1930.
22. Letter from Archie Rice in the *New York Sun*, May 28, 1918.
23. Alfred Skinner (note 19) suggested Berkeley or Carteret; Elmer Boyd suggested Douglass. The minutes of the first faculty meeting, Dec. 13, 1918, contain a prefatory statement titled "The Founding of the New Jersey College for Women."
24. Letter, Douglass to Mrs. Marvin, Jan. 25, 1915; news release April, 1913.
25. March 8, 1918.
26. Minutes of joint meeting of trustees' committee and advisory committee of the State Federation of Women's Clubs, Oct. 23, 1914.
27. Letter, Douglass to James Neilson, Dec. 29, 1914.
28. Radio talk, station WOR, Newark, Oct. 8, 1931.
29. Jan. 12, 1920. The records of this governing body will henceforth be referred to in the notes as trustees' minutes.
30. Feickert interview by Mrs. English, Nov., 1942.

CHAPTER 2

1. Mrs. Moncure Carpender (who, as Mrs. Elisabeth N. Greene, had been the first registrar of the college): "That first Summer and Fall," *Douglass Alumnae Bulletin*, April, 1935.

2. Annual report to the trustees for 1928, 1931; trustees' minutes, Oct. 3, 1924, Nov. 5, 1926.

3. Trustees' minutes, Dec. 8, 1927.

4. The ms., in pencil, is in the Douglass papers.

5. Talk at class of 1926 banquet, Hotel Pennsylvania, New York, March 27, 1926; Neilson papers.

6. Jan. 24, 1922.

7. Trustees' minutes, *passim;* letter from Loree to Dean Corwin, Feb. 14, 1936.

8. *Campus News,* Oct. 9, 1928.

9. Trustees' minutes, Jan. 28, 1921.

10. Trustees' minutes, June 9, 1923, Oct. 5, 1923. Letter, Loree to Neilson, Oct. 18, 1922, Neilson papers.

11. Annual report, 1925.

12. Trustees' minutes, Feb. 24, 1922.

13. The land was apparently owned at one time by a man named Gibbons, but no evidence was uncovered to corroborate the claim that he was the plaintiff in the famous U.S. Supreme Court case of *Gibbons v. Ogden.*

14. *Personal Recollections,* p. 28.

15. The six-page *Announcement 1918–1919* contains, in a typed insert, the following roster (those teaching at the women's college only are italicized): *Alice J. Aronoff,* Lewis (sic) Bevier, *Marie L. Casteen,* Melville T. Cook, *Jessie J. Fiske,* Charles Hale, *Mary G. Ingersoll,* Leigh W. Kimball, William H. Kirk, Irving S. Kull, Arthur R. Moore, *Mary Mitchell Moore,* Edward Morris, Richard Morris, William B. Stone, William C. Wells, Charles H. Whitman. Also mentioned are *Elisabeth N. Greene,* registrar and bursar, and *Emma Jobbins,* dining hall.

16. Trustees' minutes, Jan. 5, 1923, April 1, 1927.

17. *Ibid.,* April 4, 1924.

18. *Ibid.,* Oct. 7, 1932.

19. See the catalogues for those years.

20. Trustees' minutes, Oct. 3, 1924.

21. Rosamond Sawyer Moxon, *Twenty-five Years* (New Brunswick, 1943), p.11.

22. Faculty minutes, Nov. 25, 1928.
23. This information came to the author in an interview with Mrs. Moncure Carpender who recalled her days as registrar.
24. P. 22ff.
25. Designed by Hazel Coddington Gosling and Florence Leonard Alden, according to a letter of the former to Mrs. English, librarian, April 25, 1946. See also minutes of meetings of the class of '22, Nov. 5 and 18, 1919.
26. Katharine Boynton.
27. Annual report of Dean Douglass, 1926.
28. Told to the author by Professor Helena Kees, chairman of the department of physical education for many years.
29. Trustees' minutes, Oct. 6, 1922.
30. Faculty minutes, May 1, 1923.
31. The chairman was Madeline Torrens. Faculty minutes, April 26, 1927, May 5, 1928.
32. It is only fair to note here that Mrs. Moxon, in her twenty-fifth anniversary sketch, sees things in a somewhat different light. Herself a student in the late 'twenties, she finds that *Campus News* sometimes "fumed" at student apathy and misunderstanding, and that students often held passionate views not those of their elders. No doubt she is right; a participant in an historic event is aware of its flavor to a degree that a later researcher can never recapture. The most difficult task of the historian is to breathe life into the dead bones of the past and to enrich the pale drab historical record with some of the color and clutter of events as they actually occurred.
33. Trustees' minutes, Feb. 24, 1922.
34. Tabulations in the Douglass papers.
35. The specialist was Zdislava Prohaskova who had been secured through the good offices of Mr. Loree. Miss Prohaskova set up the entire program of dances and music. In the absence of Professor Kees, who was on leave at Harvard that year, most of the work of organizing and administering the event fell upon the shoulders of the student chairman, Ruth Tot-

man. Two performances were given, one for faculty and friends, one for the general public.

36. Trustees' minutes, Feb. 1, 1929.
37. Trustees' minutes, Dec. 5, 1930. See also President Thomas' annual report for 1930.
38. Views expressed in notes prepared for a meeting with the Regents, Oct. 27, 1931. The notes give a glimpse of the dean's methods of meeting forces and powers with whom she had to come to terms. "Regents want to get N.J.C. to *admit* having done something *wrong.* . . . Think of something that could be a concession to the Regents—same to come out as their idea so that the Regents could justify their existence—that would help us greatly." Douglass papers.
39. Trustees' minutes, Feb. 6, 1931.
40. *Ibid.,* Nov. 7, 1930.
41. Selected from a large number of letters of the same kind in the Douglass papers.
42. Thirty years later, in September of 1963, skindivers in that area of Lake Placid came upon a well-preserved body in the depths of the lake. It was brought to the surface and positively identified as that of Mrs. Douglass. The coroner gave a verdict of accidental death. She was buried in the family plot in Brooklyn.

Chapter 3

1. Trustees' minutes, Dec. 8, 1937; Nov. 27, 1939; Feb. 1, 1941.
2. Trustees' minutes, April 4, 1934.
3. Board of Regents' report to the legislature, 1935; New Brunswick *Daily Home News,* Jan 4, 1932; March 19, 1935.
4. *Campus News,* May 5, 1931.
5. Trustees' minutes, Oct. 6, 1933; March 2, 1934.
6. Faculty minutes, Sept. 17, 1937.
7. Elizabeth Durham, '22: "Impressions of an Interview with Dean Douglass, July 10th, 1925," in the alumnae archives.
8. Trustees' minutes, Jan. 4, 1935.

9. Dean's annual report, 1951; Trustees' minutes, May 5, 1938; Oct. 9, 1941.
10. Supplement by Dean Corwin to Dean Meder's last annual report, 1934.
11. Opinion expressed by Chester Snedeker.
12. In this listing I have included only professors and administrators who came during Dean Douglass' administration and remained for at least twenty years. I am aware that this is an arbitrary limitation. But there had to be a cut-off point somewhere; it was impossible to mention all the hundreds of men and women who were at one time or another members of the Douglass College faculty. After all, this is a history not a catalogue.
13. *Campus News*, Feb 26, 1938; *Caellian*, Jan. 15, 1948.
14. Faculty minutes, May 13, 1936.
15. Faculty minutes, Nov. 13, 1932.
16. Faculty minutes, May 11, 1931; *Campus News*, April 28, 1931.

CHAPTER 4

1. Leah Boddie, "The Organization of a Department of Student Life in a Co-ordinate College for Women" in *Deans at Work*. Sarah M. Sturtevant and Harriet Hayes, eds., Harper, New York, N.Y., 1930.
2. Faculty minutes, Dec. 13, 1937.
3. Dean Douglass' Annual Report, 1928.
4. Faculty minutes, Nov. 10, 1930.
5. Report of the Judicial Board to the Co-operative Government Association, March 28, 1934.
6. *Campus News*, Dec. 14, 1939.
7. Government Association minutes, Nov. 16, 1933.
8. *Campus News*, Oct. 12, 1938.
9. Trustees' minutes, Oct. 4, 1935. The New Brunswick *Home News* published daily columns of almost verbatim testimony, and carried the final report in full.
10. Samuel Untermeyer, as quoted in the New York *Herald Tribune*, June 9, 1935.

11. Two of them were Leonid Kreutzer and Oscar Lassner of the music department.
12. *Campus News*, Nov. 9, 1935 and Oct. 16, 1937.
13. *Campus News*, March 20, 23, and 27, 1935, March 28, 1936.
14. *Campus News*, Nov. 30, 1939.
15. *Campus News*, Oct. 20 and 30, and Dec. 4, 1937, Oct. 11, 1939.
16. *Campus News*, March 6, 1937, Feb. 12, 1938.
17. *Campus News*, March 1 and April 12, 1939.
18. *Campus News*, Nov. 1, 8, and 15, 1939.
19. Quoted and paraphrased from *Campus News*, Feb. 13 and 17, March 31, Oct. 20, 1937, Oct. 19, 1938.
20. The report of this committee made up of Dean Boddie and Professors Dorian and Schmidt, was dated Nov. 22, 1937.

CHAPTER 5

1. *Caellian*, Feb. 27, and Sept. 25, 1941.
2. *Caellian*, Dec. 11, 1941. (The date of the meeting was before Pearl Harbor.) Apr. 10, 1942.
3. Faculty minutes, Feb. 9, 1942.
4. *Caellian*, Feb. 10 and 24, 1944.
5. This summary of the War Service Committee is based on Professor Judson's annual reports from 1941 through 1945.
6. Trustees' minutes, Feb. 10, 1949, Sept. 27, 1951; faculty minutes, Jan. 19, 1954.
7. Trustees' minutes, Feb. 10, 1954; for similar instances see *ibid.*, Dec. 6, 1946, Oct. 7, 1949.
8. Trustees' minutes, Nov. 5, 1954; faculty minutes, Jan. 14, 1952, Oct. 12, 1953.
9. Trustees' minutes, Apr. 25, and Oct. 14, 1953, Apr. 10, 1954; *Alumnae Bulletin*, xxi, 1: Fall, 1955.
10. Faculty minutes, June 7, 1948, Sep. 15, 1950.
11. *Caellian*, Oct. 9, 1947, Jan. 15, 1948.
12. Faculty minutes, Sept. 28, 1953.
13. G.A. Assembly minutes, Nov. 14, 1951.

14. *Caellian*, Sept. 24, 1952, May 7, 1953; G.A. Assembly minutes, May 16, 1951; G.A. Annual Report, 1948.
15. G.A. Assembly minutes, March 10, 1954.
16. G.A. letter to President Jones, Jan. 15, 1953.
17. *Caellian*, Jan. 14, and March 18, 1954.
18. *Caellian*, May 14, 1953.

CHAPTER 6

1. Trustees' minutes, April 25, 1954, Feb. 10, 1954; *Alumnae Bulletin*, xxx, 3 (Spring 1955).
2. *Alumnae Bulletin, ibid.*
3. Dean's Report for 1956–57.
4. Originally Douglass Campus.
5. Faculty minutes, May 14, 1956.
6. Dean's Report for 1958–59.
7. Faculty minutes, April 13, 1959.

CHAPTER 7

1. Dean Adams, Annual Report 1963.
2. Federated College Plan of Organization (1967), p. 1.
3. Dean Bunting, Annual Report 1959.
4. Trustees' Committee minutes, Apr. 13, 1962, Jan. 25, 1965, Sept. 29, 1966.
5. Faculty minutes, Jan. 21, and Dec. 8, 1964, Feb. 11, 1965.
6. Alfred North Whitehead, *The Aims of Education* (New American Library Edition, New York, 1949), p. 103.
7. *Alumnae Bulletin*, xvi, 5: June, 1966, pp. 4, 5.
8. Faculty minutes, Jan. 19, and May 25, 1965, Jan. 11 and May 17, 1966.
9. G.A. Assembly minutes, Oct. 19, 1962.
10. *Caellian*, April 10, 1962.
11. Faculty minutes, Mar. 8, May 17, Nov. 4, 1966.
12. G.A. Assembly minutes, Mar. 19, 1963.
13. *Caellian* editorial, Sept. 10, 1965.

14. Dean Bunting, Annual Report 1959; *Caellian,* Feb. 9, 1962.
15. *Caellian,* Oct. 6, 1961, Feb. 9, 1962.
16. Faculty minutes, Feb. 13, 1962; *see also* Dec. 5, 1961 and Jan. 16, 1962.
17. Dean Adams, Annual Report 1965.
18. *Caellian,* Apr. 12, 1963.
19. G.A. Assembly minutes, Apr. 16 and 23, and May 7, 1963.
20. G.A. Assembly minutes, Nov. 14, 1961, Apr. 24, 1962, May 7, 1963; Dean Adams, Annual Reports, 1962 and 1965; *Caellian,* Dec. 1, 1961, Apr. 22 and Nov 4, 1966.
21. *Red Book,* 1966–67, p. 44.
22. *Caellian,* Apr. 8, 1966.
23. G.A. Assembly minutes, Oct. 22 and Nov. 5, 1963; Jan. 12, Feb. 16, Mar. 3, Mar. 9, Apr. 26, 1965; *Caellian,* Feb. 12 and 19, 1965.
24. *Caellian,* Sept. 24, 1965.
25. *Caellian,* Apr. 29, 1966.
26. Eugene Genovese, associate professor of history at Rutgers; James Mellen, co-director of the Free University of New York.
27. *Caellian,* Sept. 17 and 24, Oct. 1, 8, 15, 1965; Apr. 29, 1966.
28. *Caellian,* Sept. 10, 1965; G.A. Assembly minutes, Oct. 22, 1963, Oct. 13, 1964.
29. *Caellian,* Feb. 17, 1967.
30. Dean Adams, Annual Report 1961.

Index

277

Index

278

Index

Index

Index

Index